# Dysfunctional Families

## Everyone Has One

by

C Schiffer

ISBN: 0-75966-033-6

This book is printed on acid free paper.

1stBooks – rev. 8/30/01

# *Dysfunctional Familie*
# *Everyone Has One*

I went through the first 38 years of my life in a dysfunctional manner unaware that some of my thinking, behavior and emotions were such. Then on Columbus Day in 1979 I went into rehab for alcoholism. Chris discovered a route to the new world and I discovered a route to a new way of living.

I was a typical alcoholic - above average in intelligence, a workaholic, one who sets tremendous goals for herself that she can't possibly achieve and the accomplishments to her seem shallow. (I read that somewhere and it fit me. I accept it and you may want to for yourself, if you're that type alcoholic, or your loved one may fit that mold.) I have a decent background - seven hard working brothers and sisters who had a grounding in Catholicism (I considered going into the convent in my youth and then decided I could do God's work just as well, if not better, living out in the world). We all had good jobs back home because our father and family had a reputation and character that got us in the door to jobs we applied for. My father was an alcoholic and I was the chip off the old block (that chip is usually the daughter). I was also the hero kid in the family. Consequently, I lived at home until 23, trying to "fix" things until our family priest told me to leave and get out of the way. I left and went ninety miles away from my home. My father was the typical alcoholic described above who worked hard and tried setting a moral example for his kids. At one time he worked three jobs to provide for us. He never ran around on my mother and had no tolerance for off color jokes (I know because he called me on it when I was in my thirties and he was visiting in our home). His words to me were, “we never brought you up to talk that way and it’s not funny at all.” I always listened to my father and whenever I had a decision to make of any importance I consulted him, even after I was married. He was always encouraging, always positive, never said, “I told you so” when he was right and I was wrong against his advice. Always called me “Gal” except when he was emphatic about something and then it was “Constance”, my birth name, not Connie, what everyone calls me. (Of course I’ve been called other things as everyone has who is alive and trying to make a difference in this world for the good. If you’re not being attacked then your vegetating and not giving the devil anything to concern himself with.) Although I played a part in putting my dad into a facility for alcoholism 36 years ago. He still could not stay off the sauce and he died in his late sixties. Since most of his family lived pretty long lives (the ones who didn’t drink) I would venture to guess he may have lived into his nineties if he had been able to quit drinking.

I married and we raised four kids together until the kids were teenagers. They were 11, 12, 13 and 16 when our marriage was no longer two but had become me and the kids. During the fifteen years I was working with my ex-husband raising a family we both worked very hard and acquired a very comfortable life style in an upscale neighborhood with our two Lincolns on the drive and our 36 ft. Chris down at the shore and a very active social life. The kids had everything we thought they should have, parents who loved and disciplined, involvement in school activities, scouts, vacations, sports, in church every Sunday and Holiday, prayers before meals and sometimes the Rosary in the evening. The boys were altar boys. We had a lot of fun together and with our extended family, and still do. We are blessed. I was doing things just the way my parents did (the apple doesn't fall far from the tree). What I was sure was correct I found out later in recovery was WRONG. I don't beat myself for mistakes though because one of the best things I learned in rehab was, my parents did the best they could with the tools they had available to them and so the same applies to my ex-husband and me. So with that out of the way the next avenue to follow was CHANGE. Boy did everyone bulk at that thought. When I left rehab with a head full of new knowledge that I wanted to share with everyone in the family I was not met with open arms but rather with a look of, "Wow, is she nuts".

While in rehab I began having a spiritual awakening which is most critical in recovering from alcoholism. I had always prayed to God, "Please don't let me get drunk when I drink tonight". I was serious about this because a social life had required drinking alcohol and since my first drink at 18 years of age I was smitten by the feeling alcohol gave me, you know, the usual - I felt physically attractive, brave, and hang-up free. Of course the next morning I felt guilty and lost because those black-outs prevented me from remembering if I had been funny and entertaining the night before or a loud-mouthed, insulting, miserable wench. I felt miserable until the 72 hours passed and the remorse was forgotten. I was happy to be okay and able to take a drink another day. Of course it was never just one anyway. From age 18 to 38 I pondered, fussed about, tried to alter or control, and finally gave into this thing I was suffering from. Then I hit bottom and at the challenge of a very good friend I tried to stay away from alcohol for 30 days, failed and asked for help. She and my cousin got me into the hospital for a two week crash course in my disease. Back then a person could go for just two weeks and I wanted it so bad, I listened up and responded as best and quickly as I could. I had a husband at home who was totally disgusted with my problem and I had four kids at home who were confused and worried to death about their mother. The youngest of which was the one who said the magic words the morning I went into rehab. He said with tears in his eyes, "Mom you drink too much and I don't want you to die." That was the biggest incentively kick in the pants I ever needed. By four in the afternoon that day I was in an alcohol recovery unit in the hospital.

Two days before I was to leave the hospital my counselor informed me that I was not going to make it because I did not have the gut feeling to which I asked, "What's the gut feeling"? She told me the answer was God. That night when I went to bed I prayed, "God, make me sober." Now that was quite a different prayer than the one I always prayed about not letting me get drunk when I drank. I left the hospital and then my life got really difficult.

I was told to hit 90 meetings in 90 days. That was a big order for someone who had a job to maintain, four kids to raise, a big house to keep cleaned and stocked with food, kids activities after and during school, and a husband who was acting strange. I did not know that he had begun using cocaine with his friends. It was the 80's now and a lot of those who could afford it were experimenting with this drug.

There were meetings every day, all day, in our county. Since I did not know my way around except to work, grocery stores, mall, church and schools, I was really nervous about driving to these meetings, where I had never driven before. I would look up a meeting in the AA (Alcoholics Anonymous) Meeting Schedule Book, call the police station in that town for directions, get in my car and drive, praying all the way that God would get me to the meeting. In the two years of attending meetings in the state where we lived I was never lost nor was I ever late for a meeting.

I was told to get a sponsor, so I got a sponsor. I

was told never to say NO when asked to do something and so I did what I was asked to do. Consequently my recovery was swift, even while my head was working very hard to clear up. I was told it would take six months to get my brains unscrambled and two years to get them out of hock. They were right.

During those two years my husband was using cocaine more and more and staying away from the house more and for longer periods of time. This was completely out of character for him. He had always been a very attentive husband and father, a great provider and protector, a leader in all areas. Now he was a total stranger, leaving for days at a time and coming home and falling asleep wherever he fell down. Sleeping forever and mean as anything when he was awake. The atmosphere in our house was extremely nerve racking.

I began going to Alanon along with the kids and to the local university for a seminar on “Getting in Touch With Your Feelings”. These meetings helped me recoup my sanity and hold on to it while my world was falling apart. Bills were beginning to pile up and keeping caught up financially was more and more difficult since my husband was putting more and more up his nose. The kids began acting out negatively since their usual positive behavior was going unnoticed by their father.

It was no coincidence that I was working for a large law firm in the area. When looking back I can see God put me in that job for a multitude of reasons. They went to court for me on a number of occasions: i.e., truancy for one son from school, petty theft by the boys (who were still trying anything to get their dad's attention since they didn't need the money), assault on me and our son by our cocaine addicted head of the family. Divorce court and custody battles followed, and repeated court appearances because he kept fighting me every step of the way. During this trying period God walked with me all the way because I asked Him to and I found out He was the only One who would not change. When you stand on a promise God makes he keeps that promise and never fails you. At times I came out of court at first thinking I had lost but when I really thought about the whole situation I determined that through this particular instance I had grown and gained knowledge and that was a plus.

After about two years of working the AA Program and Alanon Program I had a real spiritual awakening. It began during an AA meeting that I chaired at our local hospital. In trying to get a young man, who had a very strong spiritual life, in touch with another young man, who just couldn't get with this God thing, something interesting occurred. The Spirit filled young man came into the meeting a little late and at break I asked that he try getting God to the young man who was looking for Him. The Spirit filled young fella told me he had been reading his bible at home and praying when the Lord showed him to go to where I was at and decipel to me. He did not know exactly where the meeting was that I was chairing, just an approximate, but God led him to the place. When I introduced the two guys to each other the one who needed God could not stay after the meeting because he had to get home to his wife and the one who knew God said he had come to talk to me anyway. He came to my home after the meeting to talk. He introduced me to Jesus Christ. I said the sinner's prayer with him and asked the Holy Spirit to come into my life and fill me.

This young man insisted I go to church with him the following Sunday and to a special bible study one day of the week for alcoholics. I began going with him and met a great bunch of Spirit filled people. I learned about Jesus Christ and His Word through the Bible. This began a whole new life for me. I was 40 years old.

During this time I was attending a service where a teacher was telling us about the Holy Spirit and how He can work in our lives and how He can reveal things to us in our dreams. I was being harassed more than I cared to be by my cocaine addicted ex and I was worn out and quite tired of it. The teacher had told us that we do not pray to the Holy Spirit but that we talk to Him. That night before I went to bed I spoke with the Holy Spirit and asked that He reveal to me in a dream when this tyranny and oppression at the hands of my very sick ex would end. I went to sleep and I awoke sitting up in bed repeating the words, CDS (**CDS means controlled dangerous substance.**) possession and distribution over and over again. When I became aware of what I was doing I was startled because I never talked or walked in my sleep and those words were strange. I went downstairs for a cup of hot milk and to read my bible. I noticed the clock said 1:00 AM. I didn't think I should have been dreaming then since we dream 15 minutes before waking up. I usually didn't wake up until 6:00 AM. As I sat there a dream I had dreamt became extremely vivid to me. I dreamt I was face to face with a figure who was dressed in a purple robe with a cinch around the waist. The figure had white shoulder length hair. I couldn't distinguish the face. The person had a menorah in hand. It was dark blue with red berries and silver trim. The seventh candle holder on the menorah had a hinge and it was able to be manipulated by the one holding it - pretty neat. I could distinguish the back of my ex between me and the person. My ex had a talent for inventing things that always amazed me. He was extremely mechanically inventive. Suddenly, a rectangularly shaped sign (white with black letters) kept flashing in place of the vision and it read CDS Possession and Distribution. It kept flashing and I woke up repeating the words while sitting up in my bed.

I Went to my next bible study and asked a friend what the dream meant and he told me to read the Book of Daniel. I asked another person and he told me to read the Book of Revelation. When I got home from bible study I began reading Revelations and there in the twelfth verse was described the vision I had seen in my dream. I had never read Revelations before. When I read Daniel I kept learning over and over again about faith. After that experience at 1:00 AM I was awakened many times at 1:00 AM and I knew to go right to scripture because God would reveal something to me that I would need the next day. I was truly blessed because I had a guide to get me through those dark days. Quite frequently God would use the voice of one of my children to wake me up. When my kids called I always ran and God knows his people very well and all their thoughts and what's in their hearts. He also knows how important my kids are to me - my four and the many others he has sent my way.

A minister told me that the purple robe meant the glory of God, the blue in the menorah meant the Holy Spirit, the red of the berries on the menorah signified the blood of Christ and the silver trim meant redemption. He also told me to go to the Revelation and read about the seven churches, the seventh being Laodicea and I did. I then knew He was telling me about my ex and that the tyranny and oppression would end with an arrest for CDS possession and distribution.

Approximately six months prior to this I had given the drug task force in our county all the information I had gleaned and accumulated in observing my ex. His phone calls, phone numbers and statements he had made to me to throw me off track of what he was doing. My ex was mixed up with some persons of questionable character.

In providing this information to the drug task force in my county the person with whom I was communicating advised me not to reveal the information to the host county of my ex's drug involvement. This of course involved wheeling and dealing, as well as using, as is the case in the world of the drug user. Using and dealing go hand in hand. He had warned me that this particular county was trying to get to the source that some unknown person (to them) was supplying, regarding cocaine movement in that county. I was warned that particular county would gobble up all the information I was able to supply and would ignore any need for protection for myself or my kids.

Now would be a good time to describe how I tied up with a representative of the drug task force in my county. After a time of bewilderment, not knowing what was happening to my ex, and finally concluding that he was on some type of drug, I began a class at our local high school on determining if your kid was on drugs. My kids were not on drugs. I was there because the BIG kid was acting weird and I needed some answers. Two detectives from our county were giving the course and during the run of this course I was asking some very pertinent questions. This let the officers know instinctively that I was in the midst of a catastrophe in my home. Later I was to find out that one of the officers was in favor of coming straight out and asking me about the condition in my home, while the other officer thought it best to keep still and see what else I would reveal to them in the questions I asked during the class. He was also afraid he would frighten me off. I guess my fear was apparent to an experienced drug investigator like himself.

The day finally came when I approached the officers after class and revealed to them all that I could comprehend that was going on with my ex. I was also desperately looking for sense to the strange happenings that were occurring around and in our home. In conjunction with the help of one of the officers and the investigator of the law firm where I worked we were able to come up with some reasonable answers to the puzzle laid out by my ex in his attempt to keep me from finding out about his comings and goings and their ultimate purpose. Which was of course to make some big money providing a commodity to those who saw no harm in using this dangerous substance. The irony of it was my ex's addiction to cocaine. He thought he was above that pitfall but it got him and he turned into a stranger.

Like I said previously, my ex had always been a great husband, father, provider, disciplinarian, one man entertainment center for the kids. He was a good teacher. He was loyal and true. We could always depend on him for protection and direction. He thought of me in these same terms too. (Ironically, in rehab I learned we were two people who were totally dependent on each other while being in total control of each other.) At the time I didn't see anything wrong with that. Habit you know. But as time went on and I became more and more recovered through state seminars I attended, counseling through mental health units at local hospitals and lots of AA and Alanon meetings, I began to see the sickness in that condition. It was termed CONTROL. I'm still fighting the control mechanism in my life -control of another human being that is. I have to constantly remind myself of that character defect through the Serenity Prayer.

**God grant me the serenity to accept the things I cannot change (other people), courage to change the things I can (my circumstances), and the wisdom to know the difference.**

We'll call the officer Mike and the investigator Milt. I credit Mike and Milt for helping me to maintain my sanity during this trying time of trying to figure out what was happening in my life. They were both street wise, people-wise professionals. I had always lived a sheltered life totally ignorant of life outside family, home, church, wise shopping, some work outside the home, social involvement, some college courses at the local community college and a spattering of volunteer work to get me into heaven. Talk about rose colored glasses. My rosy world had turned dark and gloomy over the previous couple of years and now while in recovery and after agonizing hours on my knees in prayer the light was appearing at the end of this dark tunnel. God was sending a multitude of people into my life to help me through this period of His teaching me to be an obedient servant and preparing me for service in His army. The people he sent to help were either born-again, Spirit-filled representatives. If not He would use me to disciple to them and soon they would become Spirit-filled as well. We were all on the same wave length - God's.

Whenever I would call Mike at his office (and he was emphatic that I never leave my name) he would take anything I said to him very seriously. If I had anything for him, telephone bills with suspicious numbers (numerous one minute calls from public phones), he would come right over to my office where I could hand them over to him or we could talk about a situation at home that was driving me crazy. Anyone living with an addict can relate to crazy behavior at home that would have one almost believing that they are the nutty one. Sometimes the calls were to have him come by the office to give him information regarding drug activities which I picked up from my ex or anyone I was involved with in their recovery from drug addiction. There comes a time when a recovering addict must dump his or her garbage in his or her recovery process. This enables them to proceed on their path to decency and it enabled me to provide my officer buddy with very pertinent information which in some cases led to some pretty substantial drug busts, so he informed me after they had taken place.

I was so blessed that I worked for this large law firm at this juncture of my life. When I returned to work from rehab I was greeted with queries of where was I and was everything all right. I was welcomed back with hugs and wishes of wellness from my co-workers upon their learning that I was a recovering alcoholic. This was 1979 when it was still difficult for women to attend AA meetings comfortably in a man's world and blue collar working women, recovering alcoholics, were treated as women of the street instead of women suffering from a disease. I am ever so grateful that we have come a long way in our attitude toward this disease in the past 15 years. My recovery was made so much easier because I worked with broad minded, intellectual folks who welcomed me back with hugs and smiles and congratulatory remarks. In fact, as word spread amidst the hundred or so employees in the firm, more and more co-workers were asking me about members of their families or friends of theirs who were suffering from the same sickness and wanted to know what to do. I was always more than thrilled to help when and where I could and I could sense a growing desire to dedicate my life to helping drug addicts and alcoholics and families who had to associate with them. My path was clearly being laid out for me by God. It was sometime during this period of my life where I prayed the prayer beseeching God to work through me to help other alcoholics and drug addicts. I had volunteered to be his instrument and I could sense His presence in my life - very profoundly.

There was an instance where my ex had disappeared for three days at the beginning of the week and not the usual weekend. I began calling his friends to find out where he was. His good friends answered my query with, "He's on vacation, didn't you go with him?" The man never went anywhere without his brood, meaning me and the four kids. Everyone was aware of his extreme dedication to us. So this was really strange to all of us. A couple of his close friends volunteered: "He's sick and he needs help." Of course I eagerly responded with some type of comment of relief that someone else knew what I suspected. And then I called this one "friend" that I did not like at all. I knew that all this mess that my ex was involved in had everything to do with this man. He answered my question with a cold, emphatic statement: "He's on vacation." No regard for me and the kids from this slug. I promptly went to my investigator buddy Milt to mull over these responses from my ex's friends. He advised me that my ex would probably call within 15 minutes because the slug probably jumped on the phone and called him wherever he was, telling him to call home and let us know all was well so we would not cast a light on his dark little life. I went back to my desk and sure enough my oldest son called me from home to report that his dad had called from Daytona Beach, FL. (Like it was a matter of fact little occurrence that he went there for the Daytona 500. Like, "O, I forget to tell you that I was going away with my coke snorting girlfriend to Homestead, FL, to make a buy and bring it up north to our friends and acquaintances who were caught up in the same hell hole of mindless activity.")

When the boss (ex) returned home from his "vacation without his wife and kids" he greeted me with an article of clothing which he had purchased for each child and swung a bag of oranges at me with Hollywood, FL, printed on it. Like we should all be happy with this breadwinner returning home from the hunt with his treasure trove of goodies for us. It sure didn't take a brain buster to conclude that this guy was out of touch with reality. I struggled to maintain my cool and repress the anger that was welling up inside of me. I threw at him this statement and I meant every word of it: "I know where you've been and what you're doing. If you don't stop it and get rid of those friends you're hooked up with in this, then I will divorce you and turn you in." I beseeched him with, "What if someone dies on the stuff you're providing them, how do you live with yourself. Mortgages are being lost because of that stuff (meaning cocaine), kids are losing their parents and homes." I could see in his eyes the man I was married to for 14 years was gone and this guy was a stranger and not the man I had hooked up with. So he DIDN'T AND I DID (divorce him and turn him in that is) but not without much soul searching and many, many attempts to force him into rehab.

The week following his return from Florida I began looking over his car very carefully whenever he was in the shower to see if I could find out how he transported the stuff. As I was peering down behind the bumper I noticed a metal box type structure that seemed to be a part of the bumper but it was shiny metal like the type he had sheets of in the garage. (His garage was a fully equipped garage because he was always tinkering with motors and things. He was rebuilding a 29 Chrysler. His garage was so equipped he even had a tire balancing machine. His work area was meticulously clean. He was a perfectionist and a neat-nik and extremely clean conscious. He invented a couple of things in the past which he should have patented. He was an inventive and creative person. God had blessed him with a wonderful gift.) I went to my friend Milt and investigator and gave him the news of my discovery. His response was negative. He never heard of anyone transporting illegal contraband in the bumper. So I drew him a picture and asked him to go out and check other cars of this make and year to see if the bumpers had the same type structure built in back of them. He did that and came back with the report - Nope.

That week I watched his comings and goings with my eye on the box. The first evening while he was in the shower I ran my hand over the box and noticed screws sticking out with a bolt on each of them that I would be able to unscrew and allow a panel to drop open. He had come home late still in his dirty work clothes. I was sure he had provided stuff to the guys who worked at the bottom of the work ethic and the Spanish speaking community (he had taken to using Spanish phrases and told me he had seen Aveeta five times on Broadway - unusual wouldn't you say.) He had Colombian friends - some good and some bad - just as in all things. The following morning after an all night out in his disco clothes I checked the box and the screws and bolts were the same. I surmised he had provided what the disco friends needed. The next morning after an all night out in his three piece white suit I checked the box and the screws were turned around. My fingers could feel the round smooth shape of the heads of the screws indicating the job was done, the box empty and the screws turned around. He had serviced his friends at the top of the work ethic. The guys in the elite part of town so to speak. When I commented to him on the misuse of God's gift of inventiveness which he at one time used for good and was now using for evil, making reference to the box he built into the bumper of his car, he denied it. Told me I was crazy. That was something I heard a lot. There were times he almost had me believing I was but then anyone living with an addict can identify with that. The next time I checked to see if the box was there to affirm my sanity it was gone. O well...

I learned a lot of what my ex was doing from his own mouth. Many were the mornings I would come downstairs and find him sleeping in various spots in the house, always on the floor and often with his head in a corner. One time he was awake and watching TV when I came down from bed to check on things and he began talking and he talked until 7:00 AM. I listened until I had to get dressed and go to work. I went straight to Milt the investigator and shared this news with him. Milt told me he was still high on cocaine and in a very talkative state and that he would then go into a long sleep period after being up probably two days. This would happen every so often and he would reveal things to me that he would forget later. When I reminded him of what he said, of course I was the screwball. But I was able to put bits and pieces together and come up with some semblance of reason to his actions. Intertwined was the pain from his childhood which he never resolved and the entire ball of wax was (you got it) my fault.

There was an occasion when he had slept on the couch and when he got up and went upstairs to shower my youngest son came to me with a bag of brown powder that he said he found between the cushions when his dad got up. This had fallen out of his pocket and I took it and flushed it down the toilet. The next day when I called Mike, my detective friend, he told me it sounded like Mexican Heroin from my description. A couple days later my ex got up the nerve to ask what happened to a bag of stuff he had purchased at the health food store. I retorted, "If they're selling that stuff at the health food store it won't be long before they're shut down." And then I told him I flushed it. He was really angry and said he'd take it out of my grocery money. I told him he'd be taking it out for a long time since Mike informed me that the amount probably had a street value of several hundred dollars.

On another occasion I woke up in the small hours of the morning and low and behold I found my ex's brief case left carelessly on the love seat in the foyer. He had taken to sleeping with it on his chest with his arms crossed over it or on the floor beside him with his hand on it (makes you really wonder what's in it when it demands such closeness). When he was in the shower I looked in. There were small zip lock baggies of white stuff. I took some out of a couple of the bags, put the stuff in a baggy of my own and scotch taped it inside the waist band of my panties. I was in my nightgown so my choices of where to stash this stuff were limited. My oldest son was sleeping on the couch in front of the TV and I woke him and asked his opinion. He informed me that it looked like what he heard cocaine described as and went looking for a camera to take a picture of the contents of his dad's briefcase.

The next day I'm driving down the parkway with this stuff taped inside my panties and I take it to one of the attorneys, who by this time knew about all the goings on in my house. He told me go straight to the ladies room and flush it. I took it instead to Milt and he told me the same thing. I called Mike and he told me to do the same. He said if he came to the firm to get it from me he would have to arrest me for possession. My lawyer friend and Milt told me the firm could be in trouble for having it on the premises. All that trouble to get this stuff and the paranoia I suffered driving down the turnpike with it (I was sure every car behind me was following me because they knew) and these guys are all telling me to flush it. That's beat. But I did what they said. When I got home that evening the phone rang repeatedly for my ex. The frantic voice of the slug on the other end inquiring about my ex's whereabouts and his behavior after speaking with the slug led me to believe I messed up something for him by tampering with those little baggies. "They're light, you say - pshaw." So my little detective work was not a waste after all. Maybe the guys working with me didn't want what I went to all the trouble to get but the ex and his slug friend were sure nervous because the buyers were paying for something they weren't getting. O well - let the buyer beware.

One thing that really infuriated me when I discovered it was the knowledge that the ex was using the oldest son for courier. The oldest boy was working for his father (when his father was still able to maintain his job). Father would give son an envelope and tell him to deliver it to so and so (the slug). Our oldest son would obediently do as his father requested. One day he told me his dad would tell him to deliver these envelopes with a really strong order not to open them. Now in the first place our children had better manners than to open other peoples mail. They were raised with a moral code of ethics and they are very polite young men and woman. When I talked this over with Mike the detective he informed me that my oldest son was being used, without him knowing it, to deliver the money.

At the first opportunity I forbade my son to run errands of this nature for his father. Of course I had to tell him what I surmised he was being used for. So I explained the slug had given his dad x-amount of money which dad had taken to Florida to make a buy. Which he did and brought the cocaine up north and they were selling it for profit. I labored and suffered over having to reveal this information to my son. After all, this was his father, his hero and now he was fallen from grace very badly. I prayed, "God please let me know that I'm on the right path and not destroying someone's reputation by slander." My phone rang at work and it was my ex demanding to know why I told our son that the slug gave him $20,000 to make a buy in Florida." I replied, "Thank you," to which he asked, "For what?" and I replied, "For putting a price on your errand because I never gave our son a money figure." Now I knew that I was not imagining things. I'm sane! I'm sane!

I found this to be interesting during this time of our lives. It seemed to follow a pattern that wherever my ex was doing damage with his drug activities God was bringing me and the kids and our associates right behind with a broom, so to speak, to clean up the mess and undo the damage. The town where he was dealing and where his coke snorting girl friend lived was the town where God led us to a church where I was water baptized and I began the trek through many churches looking for and finding the truth. I had become very angry with my strict Catholic upbringing and totally disgruntled with the pastor of my parish who I considered money hungry and cold to the poor and minorities. I stayed in this church until it split. But during my time attending this church I learned about the Holy Spirit and how we should talk to Him and how He will reveal things to us in our dreams. I witnessed an instance of speaking in tongues that occurred in just such a manner that there is no doubt in my mind that speaking in tongues is alive and well. I don't have that particular gift but I do have gifts from

God and I do not doubt that gift at all. This church body, as each and every church body that God took me through, helped me on my journey. In the end I came to realize that all churches make mistakes. We are to keep our eyes on God and not on the man. I am attending the Catholic Church once again and now I'm at peace since finding understanding. I must say that my strict parochial school and home training are the reason I'm sober today and still alive. We always return to our roots. The Bible says, "Train up a child in the way he should go and if he strays from the path, he will return." I found this true in my life and in the life of my kids.

As time went on in this cocaine addiction atmosphere, things became increasingly difficult in dealing with my husband. His behavior was becoming violent. One time he came home from an all nighter and ordered the kids to clean and wash his car. The youngest son refused. All the kids had become intolerant of his demands after being gone for longer and longer periods of time. At this refusal my husband went after my son into the dining room where they were at opposing sides of the table doing a cat and mouse thing. My son was between the table and glass breakfront. My husband grabbed the table and rammed it into my son's stomach simultaneously backing him up against the breakfront. My son was screaming for me and when I ran into the dining room and saw the dangerous and seriousness of the situation

I ordered my husband to drop the table which he did, running from the room. My son was so shook by this altercation I decided there and then we would go into court and I charged him with assault.

My son labored over going to court against his father but with much encouragement from me and his lawyer he mustered the courage to go to court in case we needed him to testify. It was an evening session and it was late evening before our case came before the judge. My husband and I each gave our version of what transpired. The judge to my horror in front of my son ruled innocent. His statement, "Throwing the dining room table at a son does not constitute assault and battery," threw my youngest into an emotional tailspin. The kid was in court until late and he had to get up for school the next day. He thought the big judge in the black robe was going to save his father's life by ordering him into rehab since we managed to bring out in testimony his addiction. He had told some of his friends what he was going to do that evening. He had no idea he would be taunted by his friends for doing what he had done. Instead of being met with sympathy from his friends he was hit with meanness. This would usher in a downhill trend for this kid. When I queried my Attorney about this absurd comment, his reply was, "Now we know what kind of a father he is." My attorney then said to me, "See that coffee mug on his bench?" My reply was in the affirmative and my lawyer said, "It's full of booze, that judge should be in your Program of AA and his drinking is no secret."

Shortly after this incident another occurred where my husband ended an argument by throwing the toaster at me. It hit and bruised my leg and I used this crisis to hopefully make a difference. I called the police. I was fortunate, they were sympathetic to me and my husband was charged. A few weeks later my husband informed me that he had paid a friend to say he was on the back porch and saw the whole thing and that it didn't happen the way I testified but just the opposite. When I went to work the next day and relayed this information to the attorney who was handling this for me his response was to the effect that it was time to get this matter out of criminal court and into divorce court. He had said to me that my efforts for the past year and a half of trying to force my husband into rehab were noble in deed but enough. Someone's going to get hurt seriously. I asked him what to do. He told me to take all that information in my head into an empty office, close the door, pick up the phone, call the drug task force in the county where most of the activity was taking place and tell them everything I know.

I went to an empty office and closed the door. The words Mike my detective friend had always used in warning for my own protection would come back to haunt me in the next few hours. He had warned me that an opposing drug task force in the county where most of my husbands activities were going on would like to find out who I was to get all the information I had. Mike warned that once they got everything they wanted they would drop me like a hot potato and never concern themselves with my safety or that of my kids. That's why whenever I called Mike at his office he forbid me to reveal my name to anyone and only reply as a friend.

I got a man on the phone when I called. I still remember his name to this day but I choose not to use it. I proceeded to tell him who I was and gave him names, dates, telephone numbers, and whatever else I had stored up in my head that might help him. He informed me that from his office at that moment his binoculars were trained on the house of my husbands girl friend. They had been watching her place for a while because it was a known drug house. When I told the detective that my kids were at that house with their father, he replied that I should do whatever I needed to do to protect myself and my kids because the Colombians would kill us for less than $2,000.

This was when I reached up to Jesus Christ and flung everything on Him. I had been in the habit of watching out the sixth floor of our office building trying to catch someone messing with my car. I also watched the triple glass window in my living room waiting for something explosive to come crashing through. Holding my breath every time I put the key in the door or turned the ignition. Wondering if my kids were all right. Now with the words from this man, my worst fears were materializing and I could not do anything about it and apparently they couldn't either or wouldn't. This was the moment of my life that really turned my whole being over to Jesus Christ. My faith walk was commencing to strengthen.

I informed the detective that I would sell the house to pay for rehab (the best one in the area and incidentally the most expensive one) but he told me that rehab would cost an exorbitant amount a week. To which my reply was, so what, since it was all this material acquisition that initiated my husband making these bad choices and getting into this situation. He suggested I wait and let him see what he could do.

The following week my sister showed up from Colorado. Boy was she stunned to see how our world had fallen apart but by the same token she was amazed to see how we were holding up and handling things. She went to AA Meetings with me and to Alanon with the kids and she and I could see the dysfunction in her life as a result of living in an alcoholic situation at home. Another sister of mine had shown up for a visit when I was in rehab. She had no idea I was in rehab and was shocked to find a serious condition in our home when she arrived. I was in rehab and when my black-out time was over and I could call home to talk to the kids I was surprised to hear her voice. She inquired as to what was going on and after I filled her in she volunteered to stay there and watch the kids until I got out of the hospital. My older sister was always there for me and she is the one I called all the time when I was in my cups, or in a black out or anytime I just wanted to moan and groan about my life prior to rehab. So my three sisters were in there with me from the beginning of my recovery and they were becoming aware of the dysfunction's in their lives. Light bulbs were turning on.

My sister from Colorado had some exposure to drug users and it didn't take her but a minute to visit my husband down at our boat and come back with confirmation that he was truly on drugs and moving in those circles. She ascertained this from the way he looked (those black circles will do it every time) and the way he spoke, terminology he used, straight from the drug culture. My husband always had a good relationship with my family and confidence in this sister as well so there was nothing peculiar in hearing her on the phone with him this particular day. He was informing her that all his friends had been rounded up and picked up for cocaine distribution and he was sitting at his desk waiting to be picked up as well. They never did come to get him and he couldn't figure out why. It was years later that I told him about my conversation with the drug task force that busted all his friends and the detective's offer to see what he could do first before I put the house up for sale. Apparently he thought the round up would be the catalyst to plummet the boss (ex) into rehab and make his wife and kids happy.

It didn't result in rehab for the ex though. He just thought he lucked out and kept on doing what he was doing. He had already took up residence on our boat down at the shore. We had a 36' Chris in a covered slip big enough to live on. It slept six and had a galley, head, flying bridge and phone. We had originally bought it to get our family functional once again during the time we were falling apart due to my drinking and our over extended social life. We thought getting out on the ocean, just the six of us, would be the medicine we would need. Wrong, we always took additional folks with us, drinking in the boat circles was worse than at home and now I had two residences to shop for and clean, not to mention that hellacious two hour ride on the bumper to bumper parkway to the shore. Friday after work and home again late Sunday evening to get home really late and up for work the next day. And on the way out the door to work Monday morning step over the loads of dirty sandy clothes dumped on the foyer floor to be washed right after work and the provisions from the boat that had to be put away to be brought back out Friday to start the same cycle.

So the boat failed as a fixer up for our family problems. It made a great place for all those seedy drug using characters to gather, and a really great secluded place to cut cocaine for distribution. In the winter months practically no one was at the marina. It was pretty much deserted. The kids went down to the boat with their father and his girl friend much to my disapproval. Father and girl friend went out and left the kids on the boat. Kids fell asleep, after a time to be rudely awakened by some crude men who were trying to take over their bunks and attempting to throw the kids off the boat. Lucky for the kids their father came in time to get the trash off the boat and prevent them from getting hurt. There's that old saying, "Lay down with dogs and you'll catch fleas". These men were of that ilk and now the ex had become just as flea infested. Needless to say, when the kids came home and reported to me what had transpired on the boat there were no more trips to the shore. Shortly after I called the bank and suggested if they wanted to get any of the money owed on the boat they had better repossess it before there was no longer a boat to repossess. There certainly was no more money in the bank to pay all these bills.

The bank did not repossess the boat and no one was paying the bank for the loan. In fact it was impossible to keep up with payments. The divorce left me with the house and the bills and the kids. The ex was free to do his thing. I took the house in lieu of support and alimony because you don't get help from a drug user. I hoped to sell the house and pay off $40,000 in debt and downsize somehow with the kids. The house went on the market. The only offer was ridiculously low so I came up with the idea of taking in boarders much like my grandmother did years ago to make ends meet after her husband died. I put cards in the grocery stores and at the college seeking students or single women who are working. I had no inquiries. What I did end up getting was inquiries from folks right out of rehab so I wound up with recovering alcoholics and drug addicts who were working the program of AA to get and stay sober and clean. Each of them kicked in $50 a week and we were able to keep the bills paid. My dad, my brother and my brother-in-law had sent me $7,000 between them to get the mortgage caught up and all the utilities caught up and everything stabilized. So with family help and new tenants we were able to stay afloat.

My house was a half-way house of sorts. We kept a low profile so as not to annoy the neighbors and everything went fine. We attended AA Meetings and Alanon Meetings regularly and we all were working at getting better. My kids began balking at going to meetings and knowing how much they needed them to overcome their dysfunctional background I decided to put notes at all the meetings inviting anyone who wanted to come to our house on Sunday afternoon after church. Just bring a covered dish and lets sit around the pool (we had a 20' x 40' pool and an accommodating patio with a gas grill) and talk healing and dealing with problems (everyone's got them - dealing with them correctly or incorrectly is what makes us functional or dysfunctional). We had discussion groups going on here and there. Just as Moses manipulated his mountain, I brought the meetings to my home since the kids stopped attending and they got help in spite of themselves. When it was too dark or buggy outside we moved indoors and continued our discussion. Spiritual discussions was a predominant topic as well as praying for each other in prayer groups.

Things went along pretty smoothly for six or so months. I was learning a whole lot in dealing with people, healthy ones and sick ones. The word was getting around that people were coming to live with us and getting better and it didn't take long for the hospitals to learn about what we were doing and they began calling to see if we could take this person or that person. We did take one person who taught us a good lesson. Our experience was in dealing with recovering addicts. This young man had used drugs but he was also psychotic and had to be on Stelizene. When he stopped taking his drug and became very difficult to work with we realized then we were not equipped to deal with those types of problems. That was a lesson I adhere to even to this day. (Do not take on any problem that I am not equipped to handle. And don't be afraid to acknowledge my limitations and say so and decline.)

Word was getting around work about what we were doing to help recovering addicts and more and more people in the work place were asking me about people in their lives who needed help and what they could do about it. Attorneys were talking to me about clients who had drinking problems. I seemed to be spending more time discussing drug and alcohol problems with my co-workers than I was performing my work tasks. It did not go unnoticed.

It was about this time that my daughter had decided to go live with her father and his girl friend. I was against it because I did not want her to be in that element. I think she was determined to get her father back and thus began a dangerous trip for her. She had no idea what she was getting herself into in the emotionally dysfunctional realm. She would find out in time. Three years she spent trying to win her father back from an emotionally sick person. At the end of three years she returned to our home and it took some time to get her to a healthy emotional plane. Anytime that she had commanded the attention of her father the girl friend feigned sickness or whatever to overrule her and usurp the coveted attention of this man - sick though he was. With the use of drugs between the two of them my daughter was at the height of exposure to drugs and the element that accompanies them. It is only through the grace of God she never became a user. She had always been a quiet, obedient little girl and now she's much the same, just grown up and older and wiser.

During the time that my daughter was staying with

her father she had gotten to calling me by my name rather than Mom. Her father had married the girlfriend (a tax write off he explained) and since I was not the biological mother of my daughter he saw no need for her to continue referring to me as Mom. I was the second wife of my husband, his first being a very young marriage and she being an (surprise) alcoholic, as was her mother. (If you don't already believe it this disease is definitely inherited and so is the behavior whether a person drinks or not). Children pay for the sins of their parents. Breaking the chain is the hard part. I determined early on in my recovery to break the chain of alcoholism in my family as well as my extended family. We're still working on it, our numbers in the battle have grown though and it make's the job that much more tolerable. I had been the Mom in my daughter's life since she was eight months old. (People quite often comment on how much we look alike - we laugh because we know that's not biologically possible. But we act so much alike and I personally think God had something to do with our resembling each other.)

All the while my daughter was living with her father, her brothers and I were concerned about her and we wanted her to return to our home. I was at a seminar when I learned about praying a hedge of thorns around a loved one to get them to forsake their rebellious way and return home. At the seminar I prayed the prayer with about 2,000 other people and to my amazement when I got home that evening, my youngest son stayed up for me so that he could give me the news that my daughter had called to talk to me and she had asked for Mom rather than ask for me by my name.

Praying a hedge of thorns around a loved one is using these scriptures to bring them back. Hosea 2:5 through 2:7, John 14:13, Romans 6:14 and 1 John 5:14. My daughter is approaching 30 years of age now and she lives just down the street from me. It's handy dandy having our houses so close. She is a great friend.

My sons were not without their trials and tribulations during this period of their lives. My oldest son packed his bags of dysfunction and went off to the Marines much to my dismay. My third child and second son I took to my brother's home where he could live in an atmosphere unlike that at my house. He had always been an exceptional student and his grades were falling so my brother insisted he live with him along with me and all my kids. I thanked him ever so much for his generosity and concern, turned my son over to him, took my other son in tow and returned to my home. I was completely comfortable with my brother and his wife looking after my son and they did him a world of good and his grades came back up even though he was homesick for the rest of us.

The son who went to the Marines would eventually be forced to interrupt his service because of his constant concern for his Mom and brothers and sister. His emotional pain he felt for us was crippling him. In time he has been able to overcome his anxieties for us. He has balanced his score sheet with the Marines and he, like the rest of us, battles hurts from the past. He becomes better and better at handling his emotions rather than letting them handle him.

The youngest son had great difficulty in dealing with this entire period of his life. He had the distinction of motivating me into rehab but he also is the chip of his alcoholic mom. He's very much like me. Of course all kids are 50-50 dad and mom but in his case his traits which were much like mine were predominant. I always was people centered and so is he. He's got a terrific sense of humor (he's been told more than once he should be a stand up comedian.) A sense of humor is paramount to me since if you can't laugh at yourself, you're in big trouble. And I truly believe a sense of humor in the face of adversity has healing powers. I found that through all the crazy stuff going on in my life my sense of humor coupled with lots of prayer made this time of my life durable and worth while. This kid keeps us all laughing.

This kid's baby fat fell off and then resurfaced in his teen years along with his braces and zits. He was a home body (one of those who did not want to go to school from kindergarten on.) We worked through this dilemma and he managed to go to school but he was not particularly comfortable there and his grades showed it. When his world began falling apart he became a real truant and then agoraphobic due to his extreme concern about his mom's safety and well being. While attending classes his thoughts would wonder to the urgency in our home situation and he would be overcome with grief. Rather than let his classmates see him cry he'd bolt from the class and out the door or not even put himself through having to make a swift departure and not go to school. I saw him leave for school and I saw him return home from school so I presumed he was attending - wrong. I began getting calls from the school and hence began the arduous hours of therapy and counseling that he would have to endure.

I kept taking him to Alateen until he began throwing up after the meetings because of his inability to deal with the emotional pain. I took him from one counselor to another hoping he would respond but he would not. But I was persistent because his well being was at stake here. The instance in court with his father and the dining room table caper would cause a real downward spiral for him. I finally got dragged into court with his truancy and received my warning to get him to school. Yeah, right, the kid was bigger than me and more stubborn than I (and that's saying a lot since my nickname at home was muley) and it was impossible for me to pick him up bodily and put him in the car and get him into the classroom. I was truly blessed during this time with the help of the attorneys at the law firm where I worked since they represented me on numerous occasions. They also tried to reach my son and break this self-destruct course he was on. They talked and hugged and pleaded with him to rise above his hatred of his situation in life.

There was an instance of a big miracle about this time with my son and a court appearance. We had to appear before the same judge who made the ludicrous statement (about throwing the dining room table at your son not constituting assault and battery) and we were afraid he would really come down hard on my son. I promptly went to church and put this judge on a prayer list so that many people would be praying for his salvation and that he would rule wisely. I asked my attorney friends if we could meet him in his chambers since I wanted to let him know how his previous ruling had worsened the situation in our home. I was informed that this judge never allowed anyone into his chambers. We appeared in court and the judge announced that my attorney could not be present and what would I like to do. I informed the judge I did not want to be in court without my attorney and he agreed. But the representative of the school (who in my opinion had not the foggiest comprehension of what kids like my son were going through - she was totally not cognizant of what was going on in the 80's regarding the cocaine scourge - and completely ignorant of this kid's severe emotional pain. In my opinion she was not qualified for the job she was holding. Cashiering probably would have fit her better but here she was holding my kid's life and future in her hands.) She insisted we go ahead with the proceeding without my attorney since we had been postponed once already. I acquiesced when the judge asked me what I wanted to do.

The judge then repeated our last name twice and commented on the familiarity of our name. I offered yes that we were in court before him on a couple of occasions in particular a year ago and I told him about the circumstances that brought us before him a year ago. He eagerly asked for a reminder of how he ruled. I told him his decision had catastrophic results which had rendered my son emotionally paralyzed, had put our lives in danger, (since my ex was still moving in the same circle of notorious characters) the IRS was breathing down our necks because of my ex's negligent duties, and we had joined the ranks of the poverty class. His face showed his complete shock and he said those words...COME INTO MY CHAMBERS. We followed behind this mountain of a man in his black robe and all the while I was beseeching the Holy Spirit to come join us in these chambers.

After I informed him of what a mess our lives had become and how we were doing all we could to cope through self-help groups and counseling he asked what I would have him do. I asked for a tutor for my son since the agoraphobia he had developed over the past had worsened since the previous court date and sitting in a regular class room atmosphere was impossible. The school representative objected strenuously at this notion because it was not affordable in the school budget. The judge ordered the tutor and the presence of God in these chambers caused the eruption of goose bumps on my body. As we walked outside from the court my son's awareness of God in the midst of this negative situation made my heart sing. God's movements in our lives did not go unnoticed by this son. I could see God had his hand on him early on and he was already given the gift of faith and discernment. But the disease of alcoholism would also manifest itself in this boy also. Just like his mom - the fruit doesn't fall far from the tree.

The next day the school representative called to plead with me that a tutor was not in the school budget to which I queried, "What did the judge order?" Enough said. My son got his tutor and his grades improved. He was really not slow at all, just unable to concentrate under the circumstances. In the safety and quiet of his own home he flourished academically. But I had a feeling as I watched him graduate from the middle school at the end of his eighth year and as he walked back with his diploma in hand that this was as far as he would go with formal schooling. We eventually had to move from school to school which prevented him from plugging in, and after an erratic starting and stopping with each move he finally dropped out of school. I was shattered since I had determined that all four of my children would go to college and become professionals. There was no money for groceries let alone college.

During the days following my success in court with my truant son and the judge who misruled and adversely affected my son I was basking in compliments from the attorneys I worked with who complimented on a job well done in court. I let it go to my head. Well a time following my success in court I was ordered to court again because my son was once again being charged with truancy - this was after tutoring and a return to the classroom. I was sure the school was simply attacking my son. The truancy officer in particular for whom I had no trust. In fact I was totally disgusted with her lack of knowledge or experience with families experiencing what we were experiencing. So sure was I that the school was picking on my kid when it came time to go to court I appeared without one of the attorneys from the firm, certain I could handle things as "I" did previously. God knew better for me though and I thank Him for that.

When we arrived in court there was Larry from the firm settling a landlord/tenant case. He came and sat beside me after a positive conclusion of his matter before the court and inquired of me why I was there. I told him and he said he'd stay with us. I declined his gracious offer and suggested he go back to the office as I could handle this myself. He insisted on sticking around because the judge was in a foul mood and he sensed I might need some assistance. I resigned myself to his insistence on remaining although I thought it totally unnecessary since hadn't I handled everything just fine the last go round?

Well when the truancy officer revealed to the court all the days my son had neglected to go to school I was shocked and dismayed since I was totally unaware of his failures and I had been sure my kid was right and they were wrong. I was in big trouble. The judge was totally displeased and his face showed it. I was about to get the book thrown at me. Larry jumps up and approaches the bench all the way beseeching the court to let him represent me and announcing what firm he was with. The judge acquiesced and allowed him to speak in our defense. Lucky for me that Larry was in court that day, and lucky for me he insisted on staying in court to "watch" the proceedings, and lucky for me he jumped up to our defense. He convinced the judge to give me more time to get my son to commence attending school. The judge was not a happy camper at all (probably hung over).

When I got back to the office later that day I went and thanked Larry for his assistance in court. He shrugged it off saying they would have fined me a couple hundred dollars and I'd have been on my way. (I found out later they could have taken my son away from me.) When I told Larry I did not have a couple hundred dollars (at this stage of my life a couple of dollars was a lot) he got a look on his face that caused me to inquire about his anguished appearance to which he replied, "They would have locked you up."

This entire scenario was a lesson in humility for me. I had gotten all puffed up because "I" had done such a good job before in court without legal representation. I tried it again and God allowed the court to put me in my place but God also sent Larry to protect me and my son. Jesus saves, He heals and He protects. He had just protected me from my own prideful self. Praise the Lord.

The time had come when we would once again have to put the house on the market since my ex was objecting to the presence of these people boarding in my home. Without their financial contributions each week I would not be able to pay the bills and keep the place stable. My salary at the time was $150 a week after a chunk of it was garnisheed for my ex's bad debt. About this time too, the Lord was showing me that He wanted everything from me - my life, my kids, my home, my car, the whole ball of wax. At first I was startled and then I gave in and gave God my home. I had given Him my life when I became born again and offered to be his vessel and asked Him to work through me for the benefit of other alcoholics. I gave Him my kids because without an earthly father they were lost and I could not handle them. But with their Father in heaven taking charge of them my life became less frustrating. (I'll give you a for instance...when my son had returned to school, after getting caught up by tutoring and counseling, he would have a relapse and announce that he was not going to school. I would sit at the kitchen table and pray and remind Father God that this was His son and shortly thereafter my son would walk down the stairs and outside to the bus stop. My mom witnessed this on one occasion and was amazed. I used my car in His service by transporting recovering people to and from meetings and active alcoholics to hospitals and rehabs, in the hopes of starting them on the path to a new sober life.

But God was showing me very definitely that I was to give up the profits from the sale of my house for the good of his children. So I asked the Wills and Estates attorney at the law firm if there was an old farm lying around that we could purchase and turn into a facility for kids to get away from the city and get off drugs and alcohol. He declined but would keep me in mind. The next day he told me of a farm in another county worth half a million dollars that would make a perfect place for what I had in mind and it was in mint condition with buildings to accommodate bunks and lots of kids. For the next year I would follow an extreme lesson in faith and my faith walk would increase and strengthen a hundred fold. A lot of my friends would also be convinced I had gone completely crazy. You just don't sell your house and give the profits away. You just don't give your house away. Ha, you sure do — if God tells you. He wants us to trust and obey. Personally I prefer to be obedient.

I met the woman who had the farm for sale and she took me to see it. It was perfect - 280 acres of beautiful pasture. Penn soil which was good for grazing. A huge house which included six bedrooms, three baths, a huge laundry room, a storage closet which held a full size freezer and numerous shelves for canning, three screened porches, a great room and dining room combined, and a kitchen which was perfect for feeding a small army of kids. She told me that she had a dream that many kids were on the farm seated on chairs in the great room and that the dairy barn was converted to a dorm with many beds. As far as I was concerned that was confirmation. We put our heads together to see what we could do. She needed $36,000 to keep it off the auction block for a note past due on it. This was the imminent need that must be met.

I promptly put my house back on the market, reduced the price somewhat and waited for a buyer. Nothing happened since we were in the worst real estate market at that time - it was 1983 and the market was real flat. Almost every other house in our area was for sale and they were all in better shape than mine. The property was in much need of attention since I had not had the money nor the handymen to keep the house in top notch shape like it had always been when my husband was well and in charge. Finally, a couple came to look at the house and after they left I ran upstairs, got down on my knees and prayed that God would sell this house so we could get busy with the farm. A week or so later the couple came back and the woman indicated to me that she liked me but she didn't like the house but they would buy it. They were one of the few people who could get a mortgage at that time.

I got double for the house what it had cost us to build it so I felt pretty good about that. Half of the money went to pay off all the outstanding debt that we had incurred and the other was allocated to acquiring the farm. Before this happened we went month after month waiting for these buyers to come along. In the meanwhile the farm had buyers interested. Each time a buyer was interested in the farm, my prayer partner Hazel, and I would begin praying and bombarding the heavens and the deal would fall through. At one point the attorney who was trying to help both us women, me and the lady who owned the farm, had ordered me to stop praying. This he did after emerging from the conference room when yet another deal fell through for the farm. Over the months of waiting for some kind of financial help large enough to accommodate acquiring a farm worth half a million dollars he'd get frustrated and feel pressured to do something to save both of us women from going down the tubes. He had his hands full.

It was around this time also that a miracle occurred which showed me without a doubt that God had His hand on this entire vision. There came a time when my back was against the wall financially. I needed $1,000 for one pressing debt and $450 for my aunt from whom I had purchased a bedroom set. This particular day, the woman who was staying with me, along with her son and their dog, called and requested I bring something home for supper since there was nothing in the house to eat. I had ten cents in my purse. (Hazel was staying with me because her husband was not treating her very nice at all and she needed a safe place to live. She was also my prayer partner who prayed away every threatening deal on the farm).

Now about a year ago the firm I worked for had rolled over our Keogh Fund and my manager had suggested I take mine since I needed money very badly. We received our checks only to have them recalled because of some tax that had not been taken out of them. We were a lot of disgruntled workers. A year or so had lapsed and we all groused about the checks being worthless because of the market rising and falling and we pretty much determined we would never see those checks. And by the way we never did know how much the checks were for and I had no idea what mine was or would be, if anything.

Well, after Hazel's phone call and request for

supper, I was shelving books in the library where I worked and I was on my knees because it was the bottom shelf I was refilling. While I was on my knees, I begged God to please provide the money I needed; the $1,000, the $450 and some money for supper. I also beseeched him while He was at it to please remove me from my job because it was interfering with the work I was doing with alcoholics. But I reminded Him that I still needed the $150 a week I was taking home in pay. An hour or so later the administrator of the firm called me to his office and handed me a check for $1,456 and change. Wow, $1,000 for Peter - $450 for Bernice and six dollars for hamburger meat and buns on the grill for supper. Later that afternoon the manager called me to his office to announce that I was being replaced with another person who was better qualified to handle a job that had outgrown me. But he said not to worry that I would get my unemployment. I thanked him because I really needed the nudge out the door to work full time with alcoholics and get real serious about that farm. I was so fond of those folks at the law firm that I would never have initiated leaving them. He commented that I was making a difficult task easier for him and he gave me a letter to a friend of his beseeching this individual to get behind us in a venture to help kids get off drugs. (By the way, that check was the Keogh funds that had finally come through. Only God could know the amount of the check I would receive and that it would meet this present particular monetary request.) I did qualify for and receive unemployment compensation, the weekly check - you guessed it - $150 a week. Praise the Lord.

The sale of the house had gone through shortly after. An agreement was made between me and the owner of the farm that I would give her $36,000 as rent for one year for the farm. The money would get the farm off sheriff's sale and it would suffice as part of the down payment to acquire the farm. If the venture fell through and I was unable to come up with the necessary funding through state or federal funding or contributions from people who cared about drug addicted kids, I would lose the farm and my $36,000, since it would be used for repayment of the 2nd mortgage against the farm and the woman who still owned the farm would have no way to reimburse me the money. The agreement was drawn up and the kids and I packed up our belongings, all nine rooms of furniture including a huge breakfront, a regulation slate pool table, two player pianos, a good sized electric organ, a lot of stuff. Then I sat down and waited and prayed because we did not have any moving van money. So I waited for God to deliver. The kids were impatiently inquiring of me how soon we were going to get going as I sat amidst the packed boxes reading my bible.

A few hours later a tank truck pulls up in front of the house. It was Bruce in from the road. He greeted me and the kids as he came in the door and asked why we were all packed and where were we going. I replied that we were ready for the farm and it was waiting for us. He said he'd move us. I asked how in a tanker and his reply was he'd go drop the tanker and bring back a real big box truck which he did and he and kids commenced loading up our belongings. We arrived at the farm late that night and we gave thanks to God for delivering the farm. It had taken an entire year of prayer for the delivery of this miracle.

Since it was Saturday evening I asked the kids what church we might go to the next day. We decided to pray and ask God to put us in the right church. In fifteen minutes there was a knock at the door and the neighbor across the street invited us to Kirkpatrick Presbyterian Church. The kids told me to go and break the ice and they would follow at a later date. Sunday morning I got up and went to service. After the service a woman in the pew I was sitting introduced herself, welcomed me to the community and thanked me for sharing the pew with her. When she learned I needed a job she suggested I apply for the one she just retired from and told me who to see. I did the next day and I did get the job. It was secretary to the senior county agent of agriculture at the extension service in the county. This was perfect since I was now living on a farm and I didn't know the first thing about farming or what to do with 280 acres of pasture land which had previously been a dairy farm.

My boss and the job turned out to be a tremendous asset to me in more ways than just running a farm. I wasn't making a big salary but the shortage in funds would simply continue to shore up my faith walk with the Lord since I was totally dependent on Him. Bills always got paid and there was always enough food for my family and all the kids God sent our way. Bags of groceries would be on my steps when I opened the door in the morning and always when we most needed them. The church the kids and I were attending was helping with the utilities. They took a very active interest in the kids welcoming them to church for fellowship and meals and basketball. In time the hard core street kids mellowed and turned into ladies and gentlemen. They all loved that little church and my kids to this day comment that this was their favorite church.

A lot of good things happened at the farm. Kids got saved, prayed, studied the bible, talked out problems, went to AA meetings to stay straight and sober, went to counseling at the local mental health facility at the hospital, played pool in the great room while getting comfortable with other kids, ate pizza on the porches and learned to feel good about themselves. (During the period of turning our previous home into a half-way house and living on the farm the Lord had sent approximately 50 kids our way for help in getting off drugs and getting their lives in order. As far as I know they are all well.) There was always that letter or phone call from far away from one of the kids to keep us updated.

One of the miracles that occurred was the source of added income that the Lord sent. I was at work and my AA sponsor, Betty, called me and told me to come home for lunch because I had a visitor and it looked like the Lord was about to answer one of our prayers. I hurried right home and there was a man with horses. He wanted to turn them out to graze on the farm and he would pay me turn- out fees. The horses were brought in from the race track for a period of rest and relaxation.

This solved the question of what kind of farming to get involved. We had considered a lot of different of avenues. Ideas that came from classes organized by my boss, the county agent, on fruit, crops, etc. were considered and discarded. Our crop was kids and now the horses were an answer to a prayer I prayed all my childhood long for, a horse. Now the Lord was giving me horses to fulfill a dream I always had and help pay the bills. We had hoped to get a contract for many horses, enough to get a loan from the Farm Credit Service to permanently acquire the farm. We went to work on that with the help of the gentleman who miraculously appeared at the farm with this wonderful solution.

About this time one of the young men living at the farm with us suggested we cut the hay in the fields before it went bad. We did not have the first piece of farm machinery. None came with the farm since it had all been auctioned off before we got there and we had no money for any. The young man, Rob, suggested I get up on my prayer hill and start praying. We had a beautiful spot at the top most spot of the farm where we went to pray and gaze over the entire farm in all its beauty. A couple of the kids and I went to the top of our prayer hill which took us about twenty minutes to get to and we began to pray and thank the Lord for His blessings. As we descended the hill and were nearing the end of the path that led to the drive, a couple of pick up trucks pulled into the driveway in front of me and this one man inquires: "Hey lady, you need someone to cut that Hay." I nodded my affirmative and he offered to cut and bail it for one-third of the hay. It was a done deal. He got his cut and we had a barn full of hay for the horses.

We had a lot of lovely neighbors in the area, but one in particular took a liking to the kids and our operation. He was a cop who worked the streets of one of the main cities in the state. He asked if he could bring his herd of cows over to graze and pay us a fee for the service and we acknowledged wholeheartedly. The kids fondly referred to him as Uncle Piggy. He was a big man with a heart as big as his body. He would pick the boys up in his pickup to go feed bread to his cows. He would come and sit around and listen to the kids when they gathered in the evening to discuss problem solving. He had commented one time about how he was so used to seeing kids falling every day on the streets in the city that it was refreshing to see good things happening with kids at our farm. We were all extremely fond of Uncle Piggy. He was sent by God as well. I had become accustomed to God sending messengers to help us on our journey. Of course, Mike the detective was a frequent visitor to the farm.

There was an occasion just five days before Christmas when we were confronted by a young man who along with his wife and five small children had become homeless. Well of course we provided them shelter which encouraged people to help us even more in our endeavor. The time finally came when I was forced to insist they seek a home with a relative of theirs. They were reluctant to leave. But at my insistence they packed up and moved in with her mom in her little house. We needed the room for all the teen-agers showing up and kids coming off drugs had no patience for small children's behavior. I really labored over having to ask them to move but when I went to church that Sunday there was a guest speaker. The speaker was a completed Jew. (A Jew who had accepted Jesus Christ as his personal savior.) In the course of his sermon he quenched the ache in my heart and confirmed that I had done the right thing in asking the young family to move in with her family. His talk included the lesson on the number seven. God's number seven is the number of completion throughout the Old Testament. And as God would have it the young family was with us seven weeks. After service one of the church members who knew I was laboring over my decision came over to me with a smile on his face. He also caught from the sermon what I had. Seven weeks with us was all God wanted for that young family. I then saw of pattern in our lives. God would send his kids to us and He would remove them after seven days, seven weeks, seven months and in some instances over the years I have witnessed seven years being the completion time. I also learned from that sermon to pray things or people out of my life. So when I had a difficult person who could not or would not fit into our structured lives I'd simply pray that person out and in seven of something the person would move along on their own. Or a stay in a place where God moved us ended in seven or a multiple of sevens. That's how I knew I was in His time frame and I would not interfere by trying to inject my own time frame. I also learned about God's permissive will and His perfect will and I personally would prefer to strive to be in His perfect will. It never ceases to amaze me how He watches over me as long as I maintain this posture. Jesus saves, He heals and He protects and I have seen this manifested over and over.

It was while we were at the farm that God sent another messenger to help with the kids. This was John. He had been a tough character with a clean shaven head who had struck terror into the hearts of the locals. Now he was a clean cut, other centered, recovered alcoholic who was completely dedicated to helping folks and he helped us tremendously. He was there to help kids solve their problems. He was there to keep unscrupulous people from taking advantage of me (I was still naive around the edges although life's experiences and a lot of prayer for wisdom would rectify my vulnerability).

There was a time when we had Sunday Funday at the farm. The probation department in the area asked if they could use our farm for this event and we agreed. This particular Sunday about 30 young people came to the farm with the corrections department and those people put together a real fun day for the kids. Games were played, a greased pig was never caught (little thing was too slick), a lot of blueberry pie was gorged in a contest, and late in the afternoon we had a lot of happy tired kids and a lot of tired happy adults who felt good about what transpired that day. There was a write up in the paper the next day about Sunday Funday and the lady who volunteered the use of the farm. I was the happiest of them all.

Another time the Girl Scouts asked if they could use our farm to bunk down after an all nighter time activity they were having. They said they would slip onto the farm, pull out their buddy burners, cook their breakfast and quietly clean up and go home. We gladly agreed to helping with their venture. I had all intentions of getting up early with them and joining in their sunrise activity. But they came in so quietly and moved around so quietly that by the time I awoke they had come, eaten, cleaned up and left for their homes. I felt sad I missed them. But I sure was impressed with the litter-free area and their courtesy. I had been a Girl Scout too until I was 16 and I often remark that I belonged to a gang in my young days. My gang was called The Girl Scouts. It's sad in this day that so many kids lives live with real gang activity, replacing the Girl Scouts and Boy Scouts.

While living at the farm, working with kids, working a job and trying to turn this place into a facility for kids, I often times felt over burdened. My mom showed up on more than one occasion and chipped in. She was always busy - washing clothes, hanging out the wash, washing windows (and there were a zillion of them) cooking and looking for food bargains. She was also moral support, a buffer and a relief having around. One time I commented to her that I needed to meet with a certain senator to help further our venture and I proceeded to enter into prayer for fulfillment of one more request. She went out to hang the wash and left me at the table in prayer. The phone rang and when she came in and asked me who was on the phone and I told her it was the senator's office and I had an appointment with him right then and I was leaving her mouth dropped open. On more than one occasion she had referred to us as Mary and Martha - one working (her) and one praying (me). It was fun.

For one whole year we lived on the farm. We exhausted every avenue we could to turn it into a place for kids. This was the year of the beginning of the Reagan Administration and funding for such needs had been cut and there went any hopes of getting federal or state funds for the kids. My request to the Farm Credit Service for a loan on my farm plan (contracts from the track for horses for turn out fees) was rejected. The farm was sold to a man who had been waiting for five years for the owner to lose the farm to him at a low price and the kids and I were told to vacate the premises.

When I was bidding farewell to our minister and his wife they assured us that our presence had not been in vain. They reassured us that we had impacted the community and more people were acutely aware of the plight of kids. They insisted they would continue in this involvement.

Back then I could not for the life of me figure why God allowed the farm to be taken away from His kids. But I could not see what He could see at that time. So we packed up and moved to a farm a woman I had met had pleaded with me to move to and take over for her because she no longer could deal with isolation from family or her difficult husband. We rented her farm with the option to buy, packed up three U-Haul Trucks, and my sons, with the help of John, moved to a remote area in an adjoining state.

This farm was a far cry from the previous farm. This one was really old and in disrepair. The boys took one look at it and said, "Keep these trucks moving right on to our home town where all our relatives were." I convinced them with the help of John to give this farm another try at accomplishing what we had tried to accomplish at the previous farm.

I thought I would be broke when we left the big farm but my attorney friend whom I had entrusted my finances to surprised me with $7,000 of my money that he had set aside (in case the big farm did not go as planned, namely, help from government funding and donations to get it going and keep it going). The money he had saved for me really came in handy. When we walked into the house we saw a hole above the stove and water was dripping onto the stove. It was the toilet. We had that fixed. Then the water backed up. We thought it was the septic but we had to have the pipe to the septic replaced with a new one. We got busy scrubbing all the floors (after we ripped up all the carpeting) with vinegar and water and then Lysol because the previous tenants had cats that did not use the litter box and the smell of cat urine was overwhelming.

We then began work on the barn to make it attractive to potential customers who might want to board their horses so we could bring in some money for survival. We painted the barn and all the fencing and cleaned up all the accumulated garbage in and around the buildings. We made it look a whole lot better than it did. We had a plain red farm house out in the wilderness about ten miles from town.

We had one stallion which we had decided to purchase from the lady who held the papers on the property. This stallion had blood lines that went all the way back to Man O War but he was also very difficult to control since he had not been broken or trained. Tending to that horse was a real lesson in patience for the kids. They also had to be careful around him since he liked to bite. My one son made him a project for his 4H club.

My kids were acquiring some real life experiences that helped mold them into the responsible men they are today. They had gone from the suburbs of New Jersey to the country side of New Jersey and now to the wilderness on a farm in Pennsylvania. I was attempting to move them away from the drug culture. But I came to find out that the drugs always caught up with us. Drugs infiltrated the farming community from the big cities. My oldest son admonished me one time with, "Mom you can't move the boys away from drugs. They are everywhere." I came to find out he was right. But going to school in this tiny community in the country was a big difference from the overcrowded mammoth schools in the suburbs of a big city. The boys have since told me that school with its small class rooms and down to earth atmosphere was their favorite.

Shortly after we relocated to our new surroundings I contacted my detective friend, Mike. He had been wondering were I disappeared to and he was relieved to find out the kids and I were okay. He said the wilderness was the best place for me for two reasons. First he advised me that a tip I had given him on drug activity in a certain city had led to a drug bust that cleaned up 40% of the movement in that city. He said drug users were coming into the station looking for help because they couldn't get what they needed on the streets. They were hurting. They were able to get some of them into rehab that were hurting real bad. He followed up that news with the fact that there would be other drug pushers to take their place. He also informed me that our new location was where he hunted every year and our work was cut out for us since the area was saturated with alcoholism. He was happy we were where we were for our own safety since I had made some enemies on the other side of the law. Some people did not approve of what we were doing - attempting to clean up the drug mess.

Living in rural America was a treat. I could buy ten loaves of bread at the day-old bread store for a dollar. We could get milk from the farmer up the road for 25 cents a gallon - bring your own jug. Every day I baked cookies for the kids and their friends who came to our house after school. We very quickly began group discussions and problem solving with the teens in the area.

I cooked and baked in a wood burning stove (like my grandmother did when I was a little girl growing up in the Polish neighborhood my grandparents settled in when they came over from Poland). In the morning I would go out in the yard to pick up twigs that fell from the trees to start the fire in the side of the stove and then I would add larger pieces of wood and get the fire going. I use to watch my grandmother cook on her stove and watch how she'd take the covers off the burners and open the oven door and close it again to regulate the heat to get the food cooked or baked. I got pretty good at it because I always got compliments on my meals and my cookies. (I had to use this stove because the gas stove that came with the house had a broken oven and we could not afford to buy a new stove.) This wood burning stove also served to keep the kitchen nice and warm since winter was setting in. This house was heated by a wood burning stove in the basement. The thing was huge and we thought we had enough wood stored up to last through the winter. Boy, were we to find out just how wrong we were.

Two of the girls who had lived with us at the previous farm showed up and convinced me to let them live with us once again since they just could not make it at their homes. They were recovering drug addicts and it's very difficult to go home again from rehab when the family is not involved in a program of recovery. The whole family needs treatment when one member is sick with alcoholism and drug addiction but the whole family doesn't look at it that way generally and they bulk against the idea that they too need help. So it was easier for the girls to live in our home where support groups and round table discussions were the norm. We were fortunate too when John showed up to live with us and give us a hand with the work we had to do. Eventually John got himself an apartment in town and a job but he was always out on the farm with us helping with kids and their problems.

For three years now - going on the fourth - kids would come and congregate at our home. More and more problems were centered around alcoholic kids and parents. It was becoming extremely difficult to find a family that didn't have some type of drug dependency. People were just good at keeping it private and behind closed doors. But ever so slowly skeletons were being let out of closets. Times they were a changing. Hence, the title of this book. It seemed everyone I met and continue to meet and talk with has some type of dysfunction in their family. Some a lot larger and more severe than others. Some have it and don't even know it since they have believed their dysfunction to be acceptable because they knew no different. Problems like emotions are just there - everybody has them - it's just learning how to handle them and not allowing them to handle us.

I began looking for a job and for the first time in my life I was not finding one. But it seemed every job I applied for in my field of expertise was inundated with thousands of applicants. The church I was attending was close and soon they knew what the kids and I were about. One of the members suggested I apply for a job at the local Job Corps Center at the top of a mountain which was 2,334 ft. elevation. The road to and from the center could be extremely dangerous in the winter time. The only job I could qualify for would pay $4.00 an hour and it would mean looking after a big bunch of kids who had more problems than I cared to tackle. The whole town, I had learned, was praying for this center. Some church members really believed it to be satanic. O great, and they wanted I should go work there. I don't think so.

But as the days went on and the larder became bare, and my funds had dwindled to almost nothing, food stamps and AFDC became necessary. Welfare helped but it would not take care of four kids and me. One of the girls relocated to a larger town a ways away where she found a job and a boyfriend. I had to convince the other girl to return home because I didn't have enough food to feed her and the boys. Our house never lacked for company though since the local kids always wound up in my house. It was always that way. To this day I always have people coming and going. And I wouldn't have it any other way. God knows when I need company and He knows when I need quiet.

One of those days when we were really out of everything and we prayed that God would provide there came a knock at the door and there on the porch was the garbage man. Now this man was always bugging me to go to work at the Job Corps Center because he felt the kids needed me. He knew that a number of the local kids came to my home with their problems and that we were all about kids and their problems. But he asked this day how we were doing and when I told him we had no food he ran right home to get a bunch of venison he had in the freezer. He came back post haste with a big box and started up the frozen steps and promptly slipped and fell. As I anxiously bent over to help him up and see if he was all right he lay there and looked up at me with those big pleading eyes and beseeched me to please go to work at the center. I gave in and promised I would go fill out an application.

I went on up to the Job Corps Center and applied for a job. Low and behold I was hired as an assistant resident advisor (in other words, a glorified baby-sitter). So this was what R.A. was referred to in the inner circles of the center. My shift was weekends from 12 midnight to 12 noon the following day. I had a dorm of 40 girls. I had a walkie-talkie to communicate with my co-workers. It was winter and real cold up on that mountain (2334 ft. above sea level).

When the person in charge of hiring took me around the center for a tour I got the feeling that he was a bit afraid of the kids on center. I had lost fear for such seemingly intimidating youth long ago in my involvement with drug addicted kids who God sent to my door so I could assist them in their recovery from drug addiction and alcoholism.

At 40 years of age my rose colored glasses had completed their dissolution and I saw life like I had never seen before in my first 38 years. After the past two years of being involved with kids less fortunate or protected than me or my kids I no longer suffered from frozen horror at what some kids had to endure. I had become conditioned to fighting the good fight and do something to change the lousy conditions some kids through no fault of their own were forced to suffer. So my shock and dismay and immobility had transformed into a call to arms every time I witnessed or became aware of a child's plight.

These kids which triggered fear and apprehension in the man giving me a tour of the center, triggered a jovial response from me. I enjoyed locking onto those eyes full of mischief. They knew they had him on the run. With a glance I let them know I would not run - so forget it.

After a couple of weeks of working at the center my little white Toyota Celica was greeted with greetings from the windows of the dorms as the kids here and there would shout welcome words from their dorms making me feel very much wanted and needed.

During those long night shifts I had begun Bible Study and AA and NA meetings in my office to help the kids deal with their addictions and to help them dissolve their feelings of self-hatred and the rejection they felt from parents who spawned them and walked away from them. I heard reports from kids who had been locked in closets, dropped from balconies, thrown away, used sexually, and been made to believe they were the scum of the earth. These kids had some pretty sick people for ancestors. Not everyone comes from a nice warm nurturing atmosphere. Granted we all have our discomforts in growing up but these kids had more than their share in my opinion. And now on center the girls were reporting to me that some of them had as many as three abortions while on center. That they would be spirited over to New York City for their abortion and then instructed when they return to the center to spread the word that they had a miscarriage. The guys were informed by the center director that if they would "behave" all week that they could have a certain house on center to screw around in all weekend. There were employees on center who were taking kids to "bed" who were of the opposite sex and the same sex as well. Drugs were being supplied to the kids on center by staff. Pretty bad, wouldn't you say? And tax dollars were paying for this. I called my congressman.

He informed me that he was suspicious of my concerns being true. Rumors were rampant about the center that the whole town was praying for because they believe it to be satanic. We decided I should remain at the center and be quiet for the time being and keep in touch with each other. We communicated regularly and then the day came when I was called into the office and ordered to stop apostatizing to the students and to end the AA and NA meetings. I figured this had been initiated by the head of security who had not been doing his job and had the nerve to show up in my office one early morning with a warning about what I was doing and to cease. I drew attention to the cross around his neck and suggested that he stop wearing that cross since he was not setting the proper example for the kids on center and was not walking in the path of the person whom that cross represented.

This same security person was responsible for a young man getting thrown off center who had begun and held helpful NA meetings for kids on center. The security officer was jealous and really ticked that the kid had done what he should have done. When the kid was pitched off the center I welcomed him into my home. He became part of our family along with a young woman who was pregnant. Joe and Nancy were friends who lived in the Pittsburgh area (on the streets). They teamed up. Joe had told me that he had slept in dumpsters to stay warm on occasion. Joe's father was in prison and his mom ran with a motor cycle gang. She left him at a home for kids but his big resentment was she had "fixed" it so he could never be adopted by a family so he was denied a family life.

Joe was always in search of relatives. (Ironically we discovered in discussing relatives in Pittsburgh that he was related to us by marriage. As far as we could determine his aunt was married to my ex husband's brother-in law's brother.) Joe had been shuttled from place to place and finally he ran away and lived on his own wherever. Nancy was placed on a bar by her father when she was an infant and offered for sale. She too became a wonderer in the city.

Joe and Nancy became a pair and eventually found themselves on a bus headed for the Job Corps Center in Lopez, Pa. Nancy was pregnant to Joe at the time. When they arrived on center their relationship did not stand a chance. On center the majority of the kids are very envious of a good relationship because they don't have one so they usually go about busting it up and this they did. Before long Joe and Nancy were estranged from one another on center and another desperate, clingy female had attached herself to Joe. Nancy was left by the wayside. Nancy had refused the abortion the center kept insisting she needed and when they attempted to put her in a half way house for unwed mothers she balked. They had taken her to see it and she was abhorred by what she saw, namely one tough pregnant with a spiked dog collar around her neck. Nancy called me and I ran right up on the mountain with the help of my friend John (remember the guy from New Jersey who continued to help me with kids) and we brought her down to my house.

Strange how we had no problem getting past the security shack (no one was in it at that particular time - there should have been - but, "O, well.") When we got to her dorm after passing unnoticed through the center she was waiting and slipped out the side door with her suitcases and off we went. No one stopped us. I truly believe God had sent John and me to get her off center because she would not kill her baby nor would she settle for being placed in a hellish surrounding. I truly believe God prepared the way for John and me to get onto and back off the center with our charge undetected.

When we went to get Nancy I had already left my employment when they insisted in putting a muzzle on my mouth and forbid me from holding Bible study and AA and NA Meetings in my office with the students. The center had insisted that I bring Nancy back on center to which I reminded them she was over 18 and considered an adult and I could not make her do anything she did not want to do. And if it were up to me I would not have brought her back there anyway. I did not feel it would be in her best interest.

My intention was to get Nancy to Catholic Social Services and get her set up with help through them for her and her baby. Eventually that is what we did.

The time came when the center called and asked me to convince Nancy and Joe to meet with representatives of the contractor who was in charge of running the center. We agreed to meet in a certain restaurant in town and these two gentlemen flew in from Houston, TX, and we had a sit-down to discuss things. Joe, Nancy and I shared with these two guys what we thought was wrong at the center. After they listened to us very politely, they promptly placated us and then warned that if we did not keep our mouths shut they would sue us for slander. We admitted defeat and left the restaurant. I left there convinced that the Job Corps program was worse than I had previously thought. I had begun working at the center in September and quit in February - six months was enough.

Later I wrote a letter to Nancy Reagan and a few other leaders in this country suggesting that they clean up the Job Corps program and put people in there who were setting the proper example for these kids. Not those who would use them for sex and money.

While living on this farm (in 1983) we had a couple of educational experiences. There was a family who lived across the road from us. They lived in a barn that had been converted into living quarters. The father was a truck driver and he was on the road a lot and sometimes he would take his teenage daughter with him. My boys and Joe would spend time with their oldest son who was the same age as my older son. He was a hard working young man and when his father was on the road he would be the man of the house. He was very serious about his responsibilities. They were struggling financially and when I suggested that they check in with the Farmers Home Administration or with the Extension Service to look into help for the small farmer I was told quite emphatically that they don't take charity from the government and if need be they would live on potatoes all winter. Now I was aware of the Payment In Kind Program from working for the Extension Service in the previous place that we lived. This program was supposed to help the small farmer but as things would have it in an article that I read in the Readers Digest it seems the bulk of the money was not seen by the small farmer but was acquired by the huge commercial farm operations who were not supposed to have access to that money. Something like the doctor who got our previous farm when he presented my farm plan after I was denied with that plan. This doctor's father held a position in Washington which would have prohibited the doctor from acquiring funds from the Farm Credit Bureau but he did get them and we did not and he got our farm and we got the boot. Oh well - I am a firm believer that God will straighten all things out. And I have watched Him do that time and time again.

Like I was saying, the boys had a friendship with the kids across the road. On one occasion I was horrified when I saw the father who was in off the road from a trip go after the oldest son with a two by four and come down across his back with it. When the boys approached the father about his treatment of his son he pulled a gun on them and warned them to mind their own business. When the boys came home with this news I was really hot. And then to further exasperate me Joe revealed to me that the old man was using his daughter sexually thus the reason for taking her on the road. This couple had five kids and they were planning for the sixth which she planned to have at home with a midwife. Their bed was in the main living area - the kitchen/dining area combination. The children were to share in the birthing. To each his own. But I really took exception to the father beating that nice young man with a two by four and now Joe's report of the father using the girl sexually. So I called HRS to report the goings on.

To my door came the sheriff to investigate the report I had made to HRS. (In the time that we got to know this sheriff better I would come to be in total disgust of this person who was nothing but a crook with a badge. This person was second in my dislike to the thugs who dealt drugs and brought about the ruination of my home.) He questioned us about the goings on across the road. We told him everything we knew. While he was in our home he eyeballed everything in the place. I had some pretty valuable things piled up in our warehouse like living conditions and he didn't miss a thing. His greedy little eyes were everywhere. He especially locked onto my four drawer file cabinet which he mentioned were impossible to come by and his eyes greedily devoured my antique sewing machine. Only God knows what else he coveted of ours. After this person left Nancy came to me crying. When I inquired about the tears she told me the sheriff told her she didn't stand a chance to have a normal happy home life because kids like her only went on to make the same mistakes their negligent parents made. He condemned her to a life of poverty and brokenness and he seemed to enjoy bringing her these messages. She was crushed. My comment to her was regarding his stupid, ignorant arrogance and how we totally disregard such garbage from reprobates, even those with badges on their chests. I strongly suggested that she set about proving him wrong.

The HRS did arrive at the neighbors across the road to inquire about the reported abuse. The kids defended their father and denied all allegations. Heartbreaking, isn't it?

While we were living in this town the boys and I were instrumental in helping set up a drug task force. Drugs had reached their ugly fingers into rural America. The boys especially enjoyed attending school in this area while we lived there. The classrooms were small and close and the teachers very attentive. This was a big difference from the hugeness of the schools they had previously attended in the suburbs of New Jersey. Kirkpatrick Church in Flemington, NJ, has always been their favorite church and Benton High School has remained their favorite school. The key element being smallness, friendship, closeness, and a great trust level. They had gone from the sprawling suburbs of New Jersey to semi-rural New Jersey to real rural Pennsylvania in my urgency to get them away from the drug scene. But there was no escaping it. Alcoholism and drug addiction is truly pandemic in my opinion.

During this time we had occasion to spend a Christmas season here and what an experience that was. The winter of 1983 hit us and hit us real hard. During the night it got so cold that the speedometer cable on my Toyota cracked in half. The heating pipes in the walls froze up and the next day water trickled down inside the walls as the pipes burst. We lost our heating ability save for the wood stove in the kitchen. The floor was a sheet of ice. My older 16 year old son was under the kitchen sink trying to fix the pipes (he had limited plumbing experience), the kids were cold and hungry and there was no oil in the tank even if we got the pipes fixed. We formed a circle around the table, held hands and prayed that God would send someone to help us. A few minutes later the phone rang. My younger son answered it and I heard him giving a litany of all things wrong in our lives. I must say it sounded quite wretched. He pushes the phone in my direction and announced it was my ex and he wanted to talk to me. I declined but my son insisted and I reluctantly confirmed to my ex that our son was telling the truth. I had not spoken to this person in a long time and I was not particularly eager to share this wonderful information with him now. He offered that he'd be there the day after with a load of fuel oil and my oldest son with tools ready to fix the furnace and fill the oil tank. He suggested we keep the wood stove going all night since the temperature was expected to dip below zero that night (like we didn't know). That night we kept vigil over the stove and he called off and on through the night to make certain someone was awake and the fire was going.

My son and he showed up with the oil and my daughter and the guys went to work in the basement to fix the furnace. My ex shouted for me to come down to the basement and to my dismay he revealed to me that the heating tapes which were put on the pipes to prevent freezing which were plugged in only ran as far as the eye could see. If you crawled into the space under the house you could see the protection had been neglected. Now when I negotiated with the owner of this farm house to rent with an option to buy, and signed an "as is" clause, she had assured me that the pipes were fully encased in heating tapes. I had taken the word of this "nice" Christian lady instead of climbing in under the house and checking for myself and I had been duped. Dummy me. Gullible too. This would prove to be my undoing and the loss of all our worldly possessions. But I'm running ahead of myself.

My ex and my son fixed the furnace and pipes and filled the tank with oil. The boys had a fun time visiting with sister. They later packed up their tools and left. Later that night my ex called and offered to repair the entire house since I was bent on restoring this old farm house. He didn't like the way the boys and I were living and he wanted to make things nice. I knew he had the capability of turning this farm house into a place with character and atmosphere. My joy was short lived as I was later to find out from my daughter-in-law that he was again using cocaine. It seems he had been off it for a while when God used him in answer to our prayer. We waited and waited for his return to fix up the place but he never showed. Cocaine had won again.

It was Christmas and there was no heat, no food and no gifts. The kids went to some friends to spend Christmas where they could be warm and fed and enjoy a Christmas Tree. I declined the offer of hospitality and stayed in the house to keep watch. Later I discovered the best place was in bed under the heating blanket since once again we were out of oil and I was tired of stocking the stove.

New Years arrived with the same dreary atmosphere. Lack of food, fuel, and New Years eve my ex calls to wish the boys a happy new year. He and his girlfriend were in Atlantic City gambling and partying it up. The boys were really disgusted. I think this was the lowest point of their lives.

The next day was more of the same. I went into the bathroom and locked the door and began to pray. In a few minutes the phone rang. It was a call from New Hampshire. The guy who owned the house up the hill next door was calling to see if we wanted to rent his house. I have no idea how he knew the house we were living in was in such disrepair. I know that he had very little regard for the people from whom we were renting. We readily agreed to rent from him and the kids immediately set to moving our belongings into the house up the hill. This house had a big furnace that could be fueled with oil or wood. Oh to be warm again.

In the meantime I was still trying to get Nancy settled into a new more secure environment. On one of the trips into town I had taken a wrong road through the hills and gotten lost. I had Nancy with me and she was in her sixth month. The roads were icy and my Toyota slid and did a half circle on the road and we found ourselves stuck across the road. No worries - we were probably the first traffic this road had seen in a long time so there was slim chance anyone would come and crash into us blocking the whole road. It was afternoon and still light but as evening approached and no one came along and it began to get colder. Nancy began to panic. I was afraid she'd go into premature labor and so I told her to sit tight and I left her in the car and trudged down the road. After a mile or so of nothingness I returned to her in the car. Then I decided I needed to go up the hill where I found a road and crossed it. At the first house I found a man who knew exactly where we were stuck and he came with his truck and chain and pulled us around and out. We weren't the first or the last to get stuck there. If the urgency of getting Nancy out of that situation were not paramount a careful surveillance of the scenery was astounding. There was a brook that was so crystal clear over the rocks at the bottom and the ice patches on the bank were intriguing. The ice covered branches of the trees were a thing of beauty as well and the stillness in the desolation of the spot was a luxurious seclusion granted only to those who had the means and where with all to survive in such an area. But the scenery was breath taking. I can still see that area today and it continues to have an awesome affect on me.

I got Nancy home safe and sound and shortly after that day we were able to get her a spot in the facility that Catholic Social Services provided where she would be cared for properly. She would be counseled to decide whether or not to give up her child. If she wanted to keep her baby she would be helped and prepared in all areas to be a mother. Nancy chose the latter and the last I heard from her she was living in Scranton, Pa, with her daughter in a cozy little apartment.

So it was the boys and me. We were all moved into the house up the hill. It was not long before the oil was gone and we began using the wood we had to keep the house warm. Search as I might I was unable to find a job. Food stamps and AFDC was not on my program for long. We were still sinking and I needed to do something. We ran out of wood and I began busting up and burning furniture to keep the kids warm. The bedroom suite that my ex and I had was the first to go. I took the marble slabs out of the top of the dresser, busted that sucker up and into the furnace it went and the kids were warm. Just when I thought things were really bleak I look out the window and see a moving truck coming up the road. It didn't take long to discover the truck was coming to our address. That old sheriff was with them taking up the rear of the procession in his patrol car and between them was a tow truck. The tow truck hooked up my Toyota Celica and took it away. My sons were furious at the loss of the car. They had gotten to considering it their car a long time ago like most teenagers do.

When the sheriff hooked up my Toyota Supra to the tow truck I informed him that he would not keep that car because God gave it to me and he could not keep anything God gives to another and I would get it back and he would see because God is good and He is faithful to His people. Later on you will see how God worked His miracle with my car.

Men got out of the moving van and proceeded to load up all our furniture and belongings. They took the boys guitars, the mattresses with the sheets still on them, the refrigerator (it had very little in it anyway) and they would have taken the pot belly stove in the living room except it had a fire in it.

Joe was so mad at the sheriff that he caught him upstairs and threw him out of his room. He then grabbed that old sheriff in a headlock and ran down the hallway with him and bounced his head right into the wall. The next time I saw that sheriff he had a collar on his neck and Joe had to appear in court. Another representative who was with this bunch of nice men felt so bad at what was happening to this woman and these kids he slipped me a $20.00 bill, to assuage his guilt I'm sure. I took it because the kids and I needed it. The reason this happened? The woman I had signed an "as is" clause on the previous house with, the one who lied when she said heating tapes covered all the pipes, she moved on her option and took all our stuff.

About this time I called my father who was visiting my sister in Texas and told him I wanted to bring the boys to Texas. He said it would be too difficult for me to support the boys there myself. He insisted I go to Florida to be with my mother and he would join us shortly. I never liked Florida but after some arguing my father convinced me that was the place for me and the boys. My friend John came to pick me up and we went to legal aid to get an attorney to represent me. I then called my brother in western Pennsylvania to come pick me and the boys up. When I got home I was met with the news that my father had died in Texas. Whoa.

Now my father had told me about a near death experience that he had seven years ago (seven is God's number of completion). He had been in the emergency room on the table dead from an asthma attack. He saw the bright light, went toward it and felt the presence of God. It was beautiful and peaceful he said and he wanted to proceed. But he was told to go back because there was something he had to do. I am totally convinced that the thing he had to do was to order me to Florida. As much as I disliked Florida at that time of my life no one could convince me to go there to live except my father. He was the only person in my entire life that I ever listened to or trusted for that matter. My father always told me to try things, he never said, "I told you so", when I tried something he knew I couldn't accomplish. He always acknowledged the various awards I received in school and scouting and he was always there for special occasions in school or church. When he ordered me to Florida I could not see any sane reason for my going there but it was there I would find sense to this past four years of God's preparation in my life.

My brother showed up with his truck from western Pennsylvania. He and the boys loaded up our meager belongings and we went back "home". From there we would go on to Florida. On the ride back home I could not for the life of me figure why God allowed us to move to the place we were leaving. There was not much pleasant about the time we lived there. It had been an experience for me in living like a frontiers person. Life was difficult. Survival was rough but we had survived. God had taken me out to the wilderness and he spoke to me very emphatically. Trust and obey and build your faith and get rid of unbelief. If my boys thought their life was tough, they soon came to realize that the lives of each of the boys that sat around our kitchen table eating cookies and drinking fresh milk held as many, if not more, rough spots than did theirs. The kids across the street had their crosses to bear in the dysfunction they were immeshed in. One of their other friends had to take on the responsibility of running a farm at a young age when his dad died suddenly from a heart attack. When we left him that young man was well on his way to becoming a full blown alcoholic. He quit school and became a man with a man's responsibilities and men are supposed to hold their liquor - drink like a "man" - right? Yeah, right. Those were just a couple of our experiences. There were more, but then there always are.

When my brother and his wife arrived to rescue us from this place where things were the bleakest in our lives, they tumbled out of their vehicles, him his truck and her car, and guess what - you got it, they were both drinking. I had to wind up driving her car when the booze incapacitated her and my son drove my brothers truck when he too succumbed to old demon booze.

So we're back home in the house where I grew up

in, an alcoholic household. My brother's an alcoholic and my sister-in-law is one too and let's throw in some pot and she also likes cocaine. Will this never end? We had walked into the final deterioration of my brother's marriage and we became part of the tough love needed to effect changes in their lives.

As far as my brother and his situation in his home I am not at liberty to describe any of that because that is his story and I do not have the right to disclose goings on in his life. That he can do some day if he so desires. I am extremely happy to report that he too is sober, has been for two years and he is doing fine. He and his daughter live not far from me and we are in touch with each other almost daily. He's a fun person with a neat sense of humor and a good heart. My niece is very special, a beautiful young lady, eighteen years old now.. She has weathered the storm of alcoholism with her own coping mechanisms and she too has a neat sense of humor and I might add that she is extremely intelligent and she too possesses a gentle spirit and a good heart. My oldest son is also her godfather.

We wanted very much to get to Florida but I was totally without funds. I had applied for welfare but that was not what I had in mind for survival. Welfare in my opinion is okay for a stop gap, something to help till one gets back on ones feet but never a life time way of survival. I received a total of four AFDC checks during this time. An old friend showed up in my life and she and her husband offered to buy me a plane ticket to Florida. My youngest brother and his wife purchased plane tickets for my two sons. My brother really made a sacrifice to help us out since he lived from pay to pay as well and he had already begun his large family. (That brother is doing well today. He has always maintained a good job, he's got a wonderful wife and God has blessed them with seven beautiful kids. They are all spirit filled Christians. In deed as well as in word.)

My friend Joan and I and the two boys arrived in Florida and my mother and sister picked us up at the airport. I spent two weeks with mom. During this time I went looking for a job. I also had to get my boys enrolled in school. Before leaving for Florida I made arrangements to interview at a rehab in the area where Mom lived and I felt confident that I had a good chance for the job. The rehab was looking for a strong female counselor in alcoholism. With all my past real life experiences I felt qualified for the job. The interviewer was impressed with my qualifications but I was missing the piece of paper, a college degree. Now what to do? When I went to the health department, a state office, to get the necessary paper work to get the boys enrolled in school, the young lady waiting on me exasperatingly announced she was quitting her job. I inquired as to the possibility of my getting her job. I really needed to work. She told me to go to the office in back and see the person in charge of hiring. I went where she told me to go and the woman I needed to see was out to lunch. I filled out an application and waited for her return. Upon her return she interviewed me and sent me promptly to another office. She was impressed with my background with the law firm. My Mom and I took a ride to find the office I was instructed to go to. When we got to the area we had no idea where the building was. So I got out of the car and hailed a man walking toward me and inquired where this office was. He pointed it out to me. (God works in mysterious ways. That morning before leaving the house I had implored Him to provide me a job to support my kids. The man I inadvertently stopped on the sidewalk and asked directions of would eventually be a working companion. He already worked for the same entity.)

I went to where the gentleman told me to go, I interviewed for the job and the person interviewing me indicated she would like me to have the job because she was impressed with the fact that I had worked at a Job Corps Center. She stated if I could work at a Job Corps Center I could handle anything and anyone that came through the door of the Job Service Office which she managed. A week earlier a man had come into her office and relieved himself in the lobby. She figured I would not run screaming form my desk at such a display. She figured right since I don't upset very easily, not after what I'd been through with recovering addicts. So now I knew why God had steered me to the Job Corps Center. Working there had been my ticket into a state job. After a year I became career service which meant I would now be paid for holidays and get sick leave and vacation time. I was making $5.50 an hour. This was hardly enough to maintain myself and two teenage boys but I was glad to have a job with a chance for advancement and benefits.

During this time the boys were living between my mom's and my sister's, neither of whom had room for us. I spent time with my aunt who had a stroke and a brain tumor. We helped each other. I helped her get through the next year and a half until her death and she helped me get established at the bank with a loan and get my credit going. She let me use her car to get to and from work. My mom had already been worn out driving me to and from work and her car was ready for the junk yard.

I was eventually able to rent a house for the boys and me but the area we were in was not a good environment for the boys. It was all I could afford so we made do for a while. The boys were washing dishes after school to help with their expenses. The money they were making just wasn't cutting it so they dropped school to get "real" jobs. My aunt bought them a truck for transportation. Coming home after school every day to an empty refrigerator had gotten old real fast and I could not get food stamps because I was $12.00 a month over the limit.

During this time I got a call from my lawyer in

Pennsylvania to appear in federal court to file for bankruptcy in order to retrieve our belongings from that fiasco in Stillwater. You know, the one where the sheriff came and took all our belongings because we defaulted on the contract on that house that was supposed to have heating tapes on all the pipes and did not, except where the eye could see, and the pipes all froze up and we were ankle deep in water which later turned to ice on the kitchen floor. My aunt bought me a round trip plane ticket and I flew up to PA where I was met by my brother, the oldest of the three. He and his wife drove me to the federal court house where I was declared bankrupt. I took him and showed him where my car was being kept and his opinion and reply was, "This is like something out of "The Dukes of Hazard".

I returned to Florida to wait for a call to come and get my belongings which I planned to sell anyway. I didn't like filing for bankruptcy, my bills were minimal but when you have no money minimal is maximum. I could have eventually paid off those bills but my lawyer said this was the only way to get out of the contract with the lady who lied to me. I believed him - big mistake. I did tell him at one point that the sheriff was breaking the law by keeping impounded vehicles on his property and collecting money for doing so. Another lawyer had told me this.

Eventually the call came and I needed to get up to PA again. This time to retrieve my Toyota Celica. I needed that car desperately for work so I could return my aunt's car to her. My youngest son pawned his guitar and me a pair of earrings that I had managed to keep. (Actually my sister kept my most valuable gold chain and three pairs of my best earrings so I wouldn't sell them to pay bills and she had returned them to me when I left for Florida.) I had bought the guitar for my son two Christmas's ago. It was his pride and joy. He taught himself to play it and he's quite good.

I went to New Jersey instead because my oldest son wanted me to take my daughter back to Florida with me. She was ready to join me and the boys. She had it living with her dad and his coke snorting wife and friends. The next day I made the trip to Stillwater with a friend and we went to the sheriff's farm to get my car. The sheriff was not there like he had said he would be and his wife informed me that they had no intention of releasing my car to me. I went to the courthouse to see the judge who was the trustee in my bankruptcy and I was told I could not see him. I was desperate and so out of desperation I simply opened the door to his chamber and insisted that he listen to me. He was appalled when I recounted to him my tale of woe and how my son had hocked his guitar to get me a plane ticket. He informed me that this matter should have been settled in two weeks, seven months ago. He also said my attorney had done the wrong thing in filing a bankruptcy because it worked in the reverse of what I had been told and in fact gave the sheriff and his cohorts the right to keep all my things. The judge got my attorney on the phone and after a curt conversation hung up the phone and told me he would see that the attorney refunded my fee and that he would make arrangements for me to pick up my car. I was to go to my attorney's office to see about getting my car. He told me to call him if I had any difficulty at all.

We proceeded to the lawyer's office and while there he called the sheriff who directed me to come to his office the next morning for my car. On our way back to New Jersey we stopped to visit a prominent farmer in the area to say hello and fill him in on what was happening. This is the farmer who very graciously had my sons over to his house that bleak Christmas when we had no gifts, nor tree, nor heat, nor food. When I told him I was to return the following morning and meet the sheriff at his office where I could pick up my car, he cautioned me not to keep that appointment. He felt I would not return from the sheriff's office. He insisted I go to my lawyer's office instead and have the sheriff bring the car there. I heeded his warning.

The next morning my oldest son drove me and my daughter to Stillwater and there we met my brother who had driven over from PA. (Now mind you this was a four hour drive for each of us to meet at the lawyer's office.) When we got to the lawyer's office for our appointment we were told he was away on vacation. Strange since I had spoken to him the previous day and we had planned this meeting. We went out side to figure what we should do and then I went back into the lawyer's office to insist that we get some straight answers. This time we were told he was home sick. We were asked to leave in no uncertain terms. While we were standing outside wondering what to do I saw someone go into the lawyer's office. We waited until the man came back out and I stopped and inquired of him about this particular lawyer and was he any good, as if I was considering using him in a matter. The man very graciously acknowledged that he'd better be since he was using him. When I asked if he had seen him just now, he acknowledged that he had. Now why is my attorney hiding from me?

I went to a pay phone, called the judge and recanted to him what had just happened. He was furious, told me to give him the number of the phone where I was and he would call me back and to stay by the phone. He did call me back to tell me he didn't know what was going on in that county but he would order an investigation. In the meantime he made arrangements with the sheriff to release my car to me immediately. He advised me to get the car quickly and not to drive it out of the county but to tow it because the sheriff would more than likely have men waiting to stop me for the least little thing. My son and I in his truck, and my brother and daughter in his truck, made the run over to the sheriff's property to get my car.

The sheriff and under sheriff were there. They were not happy at all with having to give up my car. My brother went to look under the hood and low and behold - no battery. When he inquired as to the whereabouts of the battery, the sheriff said someone probably stole it. My brother's reply to that was he's in business for himself and people bring him cars to fix and it is his responsibility to make sure no one steals the battery while their cars are in his garage or on his property. My brother was ready to go head to head with these two unhappy campers but I suggested we hook up my car and start home since it was getting late. (Besides the judge instructed us to quickly get the car and leave because he had all these people in a state of confusion and while they were in this state it was best to move fast before they realized they could have really kept my car.) We hooked up my car to my brother's truck and began our trip out of the county. Along the way we stopped and said our goodbyes to my son and he went on back to New Jersey. My brother, daughter and I went on to PA.

Now this happened on the 24th day of September, seven months after the sheriff towed my car away and I told him he could not keep what God had given to me. Look in the old testament in Haggai about the 24th day of the ninth month and see if you see what I saw. God has on more than one occasion moved in mine or my children's behalf on the 24th day of certain months. And seven is the number of completion in the old testament. God is good.

When we got to my brother's house that evening he put a battery in my car that he had in his garage and threw a charge on it for the night. The next morning my daughter and I loaded up my car with some of the things my brother was storing for me and we headed back to Florida. After I had driven for quite a number of hours I was getting pretty sleepy so my daughter insisted on driving. Now she had never driven a stick shift so I ran it through the gears while she was behind the wheel, put it in overdrive and instructed her to point the car south and keep going. When I awoke in need of a pit stop she instructed me she needed a pit stop a long time ago but she didn't know how to stop the car and she didn't want to wake me. The rest area never looked so good to us. It took her only a few days to learn to drive a standard when we got home. She taught herself - smart kid.

So now that we had my car back I needed to arrange to get the title from the bank. I withheld making the last payment on the car while the sheriff had it to protect the title from them. The bank knew the story and promptly sent the title when I sent the last payment. Where did I get the money to tie up the loose ends of my car? Well I received a check a few weeks later for a little over seven hundred dollars. The sheriff had auctioned off all our belongings and the lawyer said this was my share after paying all bills connected with the auction. Not a lot for all the things

I lost but it was just enough for what I needed right then. God is good.

My son was working hard to help pay the bills. The truck my aunt had bought them had caught fire and burned up and now we needed an additional vehicle. I prayed for help and guidance and knew I had to see if the bank would lend me the money for a car. Sure enough when I went to purchase the car I was able to get a loan and buy an additional car with my son as co-signer. The Toyota went to my son and the Chevy became my car. I was fortunate the loan officer at the bank I was using was a woman who was on her own too, supporting her children. Being able to identify with my plight she graciously assisted me in regaining a foothold in establishing a credit rating for myself again. My son and his wife in New Jersey gave my daughter an older car they didn't need anymore and we were all able to get to and from our jobs. My daughter was working at convenience gas stations and cleaning jobs until she got her first full time job with an air conditioning supply store. Although slight of build she would move that equipment around on a dolly and get it loaded in a company truck and make deliveries. When she and I got off work at our regular jobs we would run home, grab a bite to eat, pick up my youngest son and head off to our second job cleaning offices at night. We managed to keep our bills paid and make the car payments and bank payments. The kids were learning the true meaning of the work ethic.

I still wanted them to get their GEDs and college. My daughter had hung in up in New Jersey living in an uncomfortable situation until she graduated and got her high school diploma. As much as we had wanted her to join us before graduation her counselor persuaded us all to deal with her situation because he was afraid she would come to Florida with us and never get back to school to finish. Fighter that she is, she conquered that obstacle with the help of her oldest brother and his wife. The boys still needed to get their GEDs.

While we were working and struggling to keep financially stable we were not without our problems. Having been raised in a dysfunctional family situation the boys were still boys who had been around the fast living pace that had done in their parents. So they were very attracted to the scene I wanted so bad for them to avoid. They experimented with cocaine and pot and other drugs while living up north and they still had not shaken off the old ways entirely. Of course they made friends with young folks who suffered the same agonies they had. Keeping them away from and off drugs and alcohol was a constant battle. But God in His goodness always sent messengers at the right time to head them off at the pass. I was still trying to drag them to counselors because they were still shell shocked from the blow up of their family life. Divorce leaves a lot of destruction in its wake.

My daughter did not have any desire for mood altering chemicals but she allowed people to manipulate her. Her battle was in learning to take and maintain control of her own life. Being a very attractive, intelligent, good hearted young lady she was easy prey for controlling, aggressive suitors. Allowing her to experience the pain of wrong decisions was truly a heart wrenching condition for a mother to endure. But being ever ready to help when asked was truly a mother's blessing. An open door policy was one I had established years ago for kids in trouble and that included my own kids. When they left to pursue their own avenues, only to find the path led to self destruction, they did not hesitate to turn and come right back through that swinging door. My door was never locked to the kids. But venturing back out to try again was also permitted and encouraged. I still maintain that everyone needs a home base. One of her departures from home base produced my first grandchild and then two came back through that swinging door. It took some urging and pleading on my part since I could not stand to see my daughter in a violent situation. Finally one bruise too many and she packed up baby and belongings and returned home. Since welfare was not in our game plan, getting a midweek paper route for her and I was a necessity. I had resigned myself to working two jobs a long while back and two jobs I had and now there was three since she and I together rolled and threw the papers.

My youngest son had all the good counseling and interaction in sessions in the mental health departments of the hospitals and universities up north. He had come to realize to overcome his agoraphobia and addictive personality (which was learned behavior which he learned from his wonderful parents), he would need to reach out and help others suffering from the same hurts he had been suffering from. So he reached out to help a young lady in our neighborhood. The mother's boyfriend, not wanting him around (seems he was sexually abusing this young lady) filed a breaking and entering charge against my son. One day while I was at work I got a phone call from my daughter saying that a detective was at our apartment wanting to take my son to the government building for questioning. When the detective got on the phone he told me my son had confessed to the breaking and entering. I agreed to let him take my son and I would meet them there. Unknown to me at the time this detective had just set my son up. He had lied to him telling him he just wanted to take him to the government building for questioning and he would bring him right back. My son did not hear the detective lie to me on the phone stating that my son had confessed to him. My son was in the bedroom getting his shoes on. My daughter overheard everything though. A while later as I was freeing myself up at work so I could meet them at the government building I get another phone call. This one from the detective saying that my son had run away from him when he got to the government building. I went to the government building with great haste.

The story unfolded that when the detective got to the government building and he and my son got out of the car, the detective came around the car to my son to put handcuffs on him. An adult with a badge had lied to him and betrayed him. My sons had always had great respect for police officers because of the closeness they had experienced with the various police officers who worked with us and aided us up north. This was a new experience for my son and it terrified him. He bolted and ran into the swamp behind the government building. The sheriff's department dispatched their helicopter to track him down and the entire government building emptied out to witness the capture of the "dangerous" criminal. A detective caught up with him, threw him on the ground, ripped his arms up behind him, handcuffed him, put him in a cruiser and drove him back to the government building. My son, who had been overcoming his agoraphobia, sat in the cruiser while people stared at him and a newspaper photographer was snapping pictures of him. Well these Neanderthals had just caused a 15 year old to lose four years of hard, diligent work that various counselors had invested in him. Boy was I furious.

Now began a real downhill plunge for my son. He was put on probation for something he didn't do because I could not afford a street lawyer. And now his latent alcoholic disease would manifest itself. Let's kill the emotional pain with alcohol. And drink he did.

I found out much later that this over zealous detective that came to my home in the first place was a father who was protecting his own son. His son was a police officer who instead of covering his beat properly, was using his badge to bully young women into sexual favors. Father was covering for his son by sacrificing my son. This was another example for the kids in good and bad in everything. Good judges and bad judges, good lawyers and bad lawyers, good cops and bad cops, good doctors and bad doctors, good parents and bad parents, etc.

My son's drinking was becoming a real big cause for concern. He was taking his brother's car out without permission in the middle of the night, getting drunk and luckily getting back home in one piece. The next day, of course, his older brother would be all over him. Then one time it happened, a DUI (driving under the influence). Now we're back in the court system and more probation. Then another DUI and it's lock up. For two weeks my son would call and beg me to come get him out and each time I'd reply in the negative. The only way I would concede was if we picked him up and took him straight to the hospital for alcoholism recovery. Every time he denied being an alcoholic and blew up and hung up. But finally after two weeks of phone calls, and hang ups and my crying after each call (tough love is rough) he finally gave in and agreed to go. I had someone from the human services office pick him up and deliver him to the hospital. If I had picked him up he would have conned me into skipping the hospital and taking him home. He was 17 and he was finally in rehab. I breathed a sigh of relief. I am not naive enough to think all would be cured in 30 days. I was hoping for the seeds to get planted that would hopefully germinate later in his life.

Two days later he calls me. I, knowing from my own experience with rehabs, knew he was supposed to be in a blackout stage for his first five days with no contact with the outside world. After giving him the third degree he admitted he had left the hospital and he wanted me to come get him. I let him know in no uncertain terms that he better sneak right back into that hospital and get on with his recovery. Surprisingly he did, sneak back in that is.

It was about six months prior to this that my ex had gotten off cocaine and joined the family. We were all trying to mend our wounds and get the whole family well again. We were dealing with the fall out of our brokenness. It was good he was with us because during my son's stay at the hospital he was a great asset in dealing with my son's pain and bitterness. Many tears were shed and a lot of hugging took place between father and son. My other son was also a great help to his brother in trips to the hospital. When my son returned home he attended his AA meetings and worked his program of recovery. Things went pretty good for a while.

After six months or so though his meetings dwindled and his thinking reverted back and before long he was in trouble again. This time he was out drinking with a friend and after a long night of it he went home with his friend (since he knew better than to show up at my home drunk out of his mind). He had made arrangements not to come home before he went out. He knew he was going out to party and forget a broken heart he was dealing with (a girl you know). He had gone out all dressed in white, pants, shirt, shoes even his suspenders were white. When his friend got home with him, my son was passed out. The friend couldn't wake him up so he left him in the car to sleep it off. My son woke up and went into what he thought was his friend's house (blackouts will distort the thinking process you know). The house he went into was a neighbor who clobbered my son with a hammer, tied him up on the floor, took out his gun and used him for target practice, in the witness of his wife and children. Great sport in the wee small hours of the morning. After a time the wife insisted that was enough and went and called the police. When the police got there they could not untie him but they had to call the medics to come and do that and see to his injuries. When blood got on the man's carpet he picked up the hammer to "punish" my son for bleeding on his carpet but the police officer stopped him. The medics arrived, untied my son, and called the helicopter to fly him to the trauma unit of the hospital. He had a flesh wound across the chest and a head wound. When he was released from the hospital he was taken right to jail where he was put in lock-down because their was concern that his wounds would get aggravated by the jail population. Being in lock-down was probably the best thing for him since he was forced to lay down and do nothing thus allowing his head to heal. If he had been home he never would have stayed in the house, never mind his room.

I prayed unceasingly to God to protect him while he was in jail. He is a good looking young man and my greatest fear was that he'd get raped in jail. (I'd like to add here that my son once told me he first got introduced to cocaine when he was in lock up previously.) Turns out he was in a cell with a young man who was facing a murder charge. This young man protected my son and lectured him regularly on correcting his behavior patterns. When we got through the required lock up time the next step was putting my son in a half way house in another city. He stayed there and worked and attended AA meetings on a regular basis. After his prescribed time he returned home and began life over again while on probation for a longer period of time.

My prayers were answered once again when I learned that his probation officer was a man who was a practicing Christian who approached my son with agape love interspersed with tough love. He recognized my son's artistic talents and when a contest came up for a pamphlet to be made for the county, he insisted that my son come up with an idea, put in on paper and submit it. He didn't ask him but ordered him to get with it. My son did, his presentation was submitted, and he won. His art work was on pamphlets all over the county. Needless to say, his self esteem soared and he began feeling good about himself. I began paying attention to his art talent and his creative talents that I always ignored and discouraged. Back in the old days creative talents were not encouraged as were scholastic talents. Thank God things have changed, especially since my entire extended family, as well as my kids, are blessed with a creative and artistic spirit. God does send messengers and he sent us one in the form of this probation officer who did so much in saving my son. I will never forget George Krantz.

Well, during this time my ex got back on the mood altering chemical trail and left the family once again. We were not sorry to see him leave though because living with a drug user is no picnic. We already had our share of ants at this picnic. Valuables, what few we had left, were beginning to disappear, like my diamond earrings, half of the good silverware, tools, etc. I never knew if it was the ex or the son, each blamed the other and I was scolded by each for taking up with the other. It was not a good picture at all. I was really surprised that a good gold chain that I had managed to keep through all these years was still with me. I kept changing the hiding place. That chain, worth about a thousand dollars, saved us so many times. It went to the pawn shop more than once when we first moved to Florida. It got me a quick hundred dollars on many occasions when we needed groceries, or we needed to keep the electric on, or someone had to go to the doctor or dentist. I still have that chain. I intend to keep it. You never know.

After five years God is showing me that He's moving me to another part of Florida. I take the step in faith and find myself in central Florida still working for the state but now I'm a screener for the Job Corps. God has blessed me. I'm getting kids off the street, out of dysfunctional homes, out of poverty and hopelessness, out of the court system and some too, who just need a little financial help. Putting them on buses and planes and sending them to centers to live while getting educated and trained so that they can have a shot at becoming successful. In each kid I interview, I see one of my own. I see their frustration, their pain, their injustices, and sometimes their despair and I'm only too thrilled to be the catalyst for making a change in their lives. I love going to work. I look forward to getting up in the morning. I laugh a lot. I could not, nor would not, be doing this if I had not experienced the ten years of training I got in real life experiences that God allowed me to go through. This was the route God got me through to prepare me for His work which in man's world requires a college degree. God's route got me the necessary credentials and qualifications. He sure works in mysterious ways.

When I moved over here, my daughter and grandson joined me. Eventually my daughter got a good job in customer service with a well known company. She began by working evenings when I would be home to baby-sit and when the baby was old enough for day care she went full time. She's very good at what she does and she still plans to go back to school for design.

My ex joined us for a time once again but not long after he packed up and left again. The cocaine was gone but only to be substituted by alcohol. This is not unusual, substituting one addiction for another. His search for happiness will not be fulfilled until he has a spiritual awakening. So on he goes looking and looking. There but for the grace of God goes me. My substitution after I got born again was helping people. That's what God put me on earth for. And I'm loving every minute of it. I'm addicted to helping people overcome their dysfunctions to the best of my abilities and when I can't, I'm not afraid to say, "I don't know". And then I do my best to help them find the one who can help them and I pray to God that they will find the help they need. Sometimes God uses me and sometimes He uses someone else. He runs the show, not I.

Over the past five years God has given me two more grandchildren. The kids still move in and move out depending on what's going on in their lives. My daughter has her own house down the street from me where she and my grandson live. My mom lives three houses down from her. My brothers and sisters come visit during the year sometimes as many as fifteen at a time. Between our three homes we handle the bedding down and the meals. We have a lot of laughs and a lot of fun. We argue and get into discussions but we have tools to work with today.

The son up north is doing very well. The son in construction has a goal - college for structural engineer and he will do it. The son who inherited his mom's disease is a great cabinet maker. He had some college in design and commercial art and he will go back, but right now he and his wife just brought one of my granddaughters into the world.

My ex has found God once again and he is working very diligently at mending his relationship with his kids. The kids have released their bitterness. They communicate, they are cognizant of continual growth emotionally and intellectually. They use their past experience to avoid repetition. Just as a bone is stronger where it heals so they are stronger where they have healed. Why did I concede to the ex coming back time and again? Because everyone counts. We can walk away from each other now because we both are on the road to recovery. Only God knows what paths we will take and how quickly or how windy they will be but He calls the shots. My ex and I can be friends and that's fine. He has his life and I have mine. We are a lot different than we were when we got together thirty years ago.

# ABOUT THE AUTHOR

I come from a large (8 children) family- hard working- responsible- Catholic school educated. I come from a long line of functioning alcoholics. I overcame my disease (21 years sober now). I have held very good jobs (gas company- federal reserve bank- law firm- county and state governments) I helped raise my siblings and four children of my own. I was a single mom from the time my children were 11,12,13, and 16. My children are married and giving me grandchildren. My job is getting young people- mentoring them and getting them into a program that can lead to their success, helping kids who are struggling.

www.ingramcontent.com/pod-product-compliance
Ingram Content Group UK Ltd.
Pitfield, Milton Keynes, MK11 3LW, UK
UKHW040016200726
13854UKWH00001B/232